Anni
Enjoy,
Virginia R Dagner

Books by Virginia Degner

Without Consent

Haiku Poems of a Woman's Journey

Haiku Poetry of a Sojourner

Haiku Poetry of a Winter Solstice

Haiku Poems of a Mermaid's Song

Fraser's Lady

Fraser's Lady

By

Virginia R. Degner

Copyright 2014 by Virginia R. Degner

All rights reserved. First edition 2014

No part of this book may be reproduced or

Transmitted in any form or by any means, graphic, electronic, or mechanical, including photocopying, recording, taping, or by any information storage retrieval system, without the permission, in writing from the author. This is a work of fiction. Names and characters are of the author's imagination or are used fictitiously. Any resemblance to an actual person, living or dead, entirely coincidental.

ISBN: -13:978-1500204020

To my husband Duane who has encouraged me in my pursuit of writing.

Forward

This novel is a historical fiction of the original Fraser family originating from Dornoth Scotland in 1757. I have written a contemporary novel of the present day Fraser family, however, I realized that in order to proceed with the next sequel of my series that I started with my novel Without Consent, I needed to tell the story of the founding family.

The story of Lisbeth and Robert Fraser will impact their family down through the centuries. I had so much fun writing their story that I regret that I must leave them now and go to the year 2014 to continue the journey of the Fraser family. Lisbeth and Robert will live on through their letters and journals. Be sure that I won't let them fade away.

- Virginia Degner

Castro Valley Ca

Contact: I'm happy to receive letters from my readers please e-mail me at: vdiggy@att.net

Who for Scotland's King and Law

Freedom's Sword will strongly draw,

Freedom stand or freemen fall.

"Scots Wha Hae"

- By Robert Burns

The carriage stopped outside the King's Tavern. Lisbeth huddled inside, peering through the carriage windows, trying to see into the dark smoke filled interior through the open pub door. She must find Captain Rob. Her father's instructions were crystal clear in her head.

Her father had received the call to arms by Prince Charles Stuart that would mean that Lisbeth and her family needed to escape England tonight! Her father's note specified Captain Rob "I would send ye to him." her father Jerome McIntosh declared.

Lisbeth McIntosh was as big a supporter of Bonnie Prince Charles as her father was and she had grown up with her father's declaration that 'the McIntosh's would walk with Charles right into the Palace'. Their sacrifices would be rewarded when Charles was restored to the rightful throne of both England and Scotland that his father, King James was denied and exiled to France.

With her in the carriage was her mother Clarise and her younger sister Letitia and ten year old Hugh. It was Christmas Eve and Lisbeth's mother had brought their entire Christmas dinner with her. She refused to leave it when Lisbeth rushed into tell her of her father's message to leave immediately and go to France where the family would be safe. Lisbeth wrapped her cloak around her, covered her head and quickly opened the carriage door . Slamming it shut she turned to the driver.

"Sir please wait here under the tree. The trees will shelter the horses." She turned back to the carriage and opened the door.

"Mum, you, Hugh, and Letitia wait here. I'll not be long. Captain Rob will help us. Da said so." Lisbeth slammed the carriage door shut and marched into the dark tavern.

The dark interior of the tavern was teeming with sailors. Lisbeth was pushed into the warm smokey interior as new customers crammed into the already shoulder to shoulder crowd.

How was Lisbeth to find Captain Robert Fraser with this press of unwashed smelly men circling around her. She held her head up, marched over to the bar, and squeezed her way to the barmaid who was busy polishing glasses with a clean dishtowel, gray with use, for the next swell of thirsty sailors.

The lusty barmaid eyed Lisbeth and sauntered over to her end of the bar, her ample breasts exploding over her tightly cinched bodice.

"Are ye looking for Captain Rob?" The barmaid said examining Lisbeth's golden red curls cascading down her back. She jerked her head toward the huge fireplace where a group of men were eating at a table overflowing with a huge turkey and all the trimmings. The ale was flowing and a riot of laughter spilled from the group.

"How did you know that I was looking for him?" Lisbeth asked eyeing her suspiciously.

The barmaid laughed. "You ain't the first one to come looking for him once he's thrown you over dearie. Take my advice and go home. You look too innocent for the likes of him." Seeing Lisbeth's determined chin up stance, she wiped the counter clean and nodded toward the back of the room.

"That'd be Captain Rob, dearie." A fat woman standing next to the barmaid pointed to the biggest man Lisbeth had ever seen. His shoulders would be twice as large as her Da's. He was long in the torso and had on a huge maroon velvet hat with a large black plume and matching coat. His boots were clear up above his knees and folded over his knee caps. Captain Rob stood over six feet tall and he filled the air around him with his energy.

The room was so noisy Lisbeth could not hear what the man said, but she was unable to remove her gaze from him. He was uncommonly handsome, though for a man of thirty he had the ruddy face of a sailor. Lisbeth sensed he was a gentleman from his starched cravat to the tips of his shiny boots, though there was a ruggedness about him. She could see him striding the bow of a pirate ship with a broadsword in hand, his black wavy hair blowing in the breeze, his exceedingly wide shoulders straining against his creamy linen shirt. His skin glowed with a healthy summer like tan despite that it was the dead of winter.

"Thank you, Mam." Lisbeth smiled and dropped a small curtsy as she had been taught to do for any woman older than her no matter what their station in life. Lisbeth pressed through the crowd pushing away unwanted hands reaching out to her. As she got nearer, a very drunk sailor reached out and grabbed her. He tried to press a kiss on her shoulder. Her scream alerted the table in front of her and every man there was up and out of his seat. Rough hands grabbed the sailor and threw him out into the center of the room where other revelers caught him and started passing him around the room. Lisbeth straightened her cloak, heavy with the gold sewn into it and marched purposefully toward the tall Captain. The gold was from her father's jewelry store, heavy ingots he'd stored away for months in preparation for this **need**.

"Captain Rob?" The man already stripping her naked with his eyes winked at her as he looked at the fetching young woman In front of him. Lisbeth nodded to him and gaining what courage she could started talking as rapidly as she could.

"I've been searching for ye sir. My father, Jerome McIntosh said I was to come to ye and ye would take me to France to meet my Da when he sent for me. His note came tonight and he urges me to come. Can you take me to Calais?"

The Captain, his silver green eyes raked over her, put down his fork and knife, wiped his mouth on the creamy linen shirt with the sleeve of it, grabbed his bumper of ale and took a huge swallow before he answered her.

"Tis Christmas Eve and I am feasting. Come back tomorrow and I'll hear your tale."

Lisbeth took out the letter that her father meant only for his eyes and shoved it into his hand.

"Please sir, read the letter, tis urgent I tell ye."

His mouth full of turkey and gravy Captain Rob took the letter from her, the red wax seal, with Jerome's signet ring impression was already cracked and opened it. Captain Rob slipped the crisp piece of paper out of the envelope and tipped it toward the light of the fire. After he finished it he carefully slid it back inside the envelope and handed it back to Lisbeth.

"Well Lass it seems that you are in a pickle aren't you." He seemed to consider, quickly stood up and grabbed Lisbeth by the arm.

"Wait! My family is waiting in the carriage" She said .

Captain Rob turned , walked toward the front door of the tavern, dragging Lisbeth behind him. It was all she could to do stay on her feet as they wove their way through the throng of holiday drinkers. Finally outside Captain Rob paused and Lisbeth caught her breath and pointed to the dark carriage hidden under the tree.

"Ye wouldn't be up to ambush, would you dear?" The Captain looked pointedly at her and making a decision drew her close to his body and walked her over to the carriage. He handed her into the carriage, looked at the three redheads with identical green eyes and hair of the girl whose arm he held, Lisbeth's mother, sister, and brother and jumped in after her.

"Captain Rob, this is my mother Mrs. Clarise McIntosh and my sister and brother Letitia and Hugh. This man is going to take us to father."

Hugh took one look at the huge man and moved closer to his mother, his eyes big with fear.

Captain Rob saw the boy flinch and laughed. "Aye, laddie, I'm a big one, but I promise not to hurt you or your ladies. I'm taking you to my ship the Molly Bee.

You'll like her and if you want I'll show you how to steer her."

Hugh looked back at the Captain and then at his Ma. "Can I Ma? Can I really steer the ship?" All of a sudden his fear forgotten he grinned. Lisbeth hoped that Hugh would be okay. Tis a lot for a ten year old boy to be thrust into such an uncertain future. Lisbeth sighed, loud enough for the Captain to hear her. He turned and winked at her with his silver green eyes and lewd smile. Then he rapped on the roof of the carriage smartly, while Lisbeth turned away with her nose in the air.

"Driver, take us to the Molly Bee I'll tell you which one she is. She is just yonder at the far end of the docks."

Chapter 2

The coach lurched forward and Captain Rob hung his head out the window watching for his ship.

"There she be, driver." Lisbeth leaned across Captain Rob's chest and saw a single lantern hanging from the prow of the ship. All the rest of the ship was in darkness.

The weary passengers were deposited on the dock. Lisbeth paid off the driver and turned to follow Captain Rob up the gang plank, guarded by one lone sailor, half asleep by the looks of him.

"Look smart Gregory, we have guests." Captain Rob rapped the small boy on the top of his head with his big leather glove. Hugh followed the captain and looked at the lad only a bit taller than he was. Lisbeth helped her mother up the gangplank, with the turkey firmly in her grasp. Letitia brought the satchel with the rest of the feast and the weary group huddled together waiting for the Captain to lead them to the galley. Captain Rob whistled sharply and out of the darkness two burly sailors appeared.

"Johnny, Jorge, bring their bags on board and stow them in my cabin." He said as he clumped in his big boots toward the galley. The mess was right next to the tiny galley and Captain Rob motioned for them to put their bundles on the trestle. "There be plates and mugs there, Madame. Ye settle in and I'll have my cabin put to rights for ye." He turned on his heel and left the little family huddled around their Christmas feast looking woebegone and close to tears.

Clarise took charge immediately sending the jar of gravy with Lisbeth to see if it could be warmed on the stove.

"Lisbeth, will ye check to see if the oven is warm too, I'll be along with the turkey. It would be nice to be able to warm it through too." Clarise smiled a reassuring smile at her children and followed Lisbeth with the turkey..

Lisbeth peeked inside the dark galley and saw that the stove still glowed red; its fires banked.

Happy that she could make things nicer for her brother and sister and relieve her mother of the chore, she took a small pan and poured the cold gravy into it and set it on the back of the stove. Her mother tucked the turkey into the warm oven and then went into the Captains dining room . The candles in the lantern that swung from above the table made a soft cozy glow. The table was set with four pewter plates and four mugs though Lisbeth didn't know what they would have to drink. Just then Captain Rob came in carrying a bottle of Claret and presented it to her mother. He bowed deeply to her. His silver green eyes seemed to take in them all in a single glance.

"Enjoy this wine with my compliments. A happy Christmas to ye all, Madame, Mademoiselles and Monsieur. I bid you good night. My man, Willie will show you to your cabin. Call him when ye are ready." Captain Rob tipped his hat and was gone.

Lisbeth brought the pot of gravy, hot and bubbling to the table and Clarise served the turkey , mashed potatoes, stuffing and cranberry sauce.

It was a quiet celebration of the birth of Christ that night. Lisbeth was relieved they had made it this far. For now they were safe.

Chapter 3

After their feast, the little family made their way to the deck and met Willie a man of about two and twenty who bowed deeply to Lisbeth's mother and escorted the group to the Captain's cabin.

"Come Madame, Captain Rob gave you his own cabin. I've brought fresh sheets for ye." He led the weary group down a staircase more of a ladder really and to the far back of the schooner where a roomy cabin took up the whole back of the ship. Letitia followed Willie with her eyes as he led the way.

Once inside Clarise sighed deeply and began to unpack their satchels.

"Lisbeth, would you pull out the trundle bed under the high captain's bed and put on the clean sheets and blankets for you and Letitia please," Clarise said softly when she had finished making the Captain's bed. The Captain favored a bigger bed than usual in a ship and she was grateful. Two in a bed was bad enough but with the wider bed it would be a great deal more comfortable.

Exhausted, Lisbeth turned away from her siblings and stripped down to her chemise. Letitia was already in bed and asleep Hugh, tucked into the top bed, fast asleep, was sharing with his mother. It was only her mother and Lisbeth left awake in the cabin. Clarise had put on her nightgown and was sitting at the Captain's desk writing in the gold bound book that was always with her. Clarise's journal was one of the daily rituals Lisbeth had grown up with..

Lisbeth bent over and kissed her Mum. "Good night Mum. We will be all right. Ye needn't worry. Da has taken care of everything."

"Good night Lisbeth. I know it's just facing the unknown." Clarise smiled and returned to her journal.

Lisbeth snuggled down in the Captain's bed and looked over at her Mum bent over her writing. She was comforted by her Mother's quiet scratching with the Captain's quill pen .

Clarise had written : *December 24, 1745. - Today we left our life as we know it and are heading for France. My dear Jerome will be waiting for us. It's come. At last the Bonnie Prince Charles is making his stand for the crown of England and Scotland. I know not what lies ahead but I go to be with Jerome, God protect me and my family.*

It was last year that the House of Commons has passed a bill to make it high treason to hold correspondence with "The sons of the Pretender to His Majesty's Crown, King James, in exile in France." *I tremble with fear for Jerome. He believes so strongly in the Bonnie Prince Charles that I fear he will risk everything to see him on the throne. Now it has come to this where we are scattering like rats in a sinking ship. I know not what the morrow brings.*

Clarise let the page dry and with a sigh closed the book, extinguished the candle with the snuffer and made her way to the Captain's bunk. All was quiet in the little cabin except the soft snores of the exhausted children. Clarise tucked the covers around Hugh who had flung them off and prayed as she drifted off to sleep.

Chapter 4

Lisbeth woke with a start. It was pitch dark yet she swore that the ship was moving. She got up from the trundle and tiptoed to where her clothes were laid out on the big overstuffed chair that took up most of the floor space in the cabin. Quickly she dressed and made her way from the cabin and up the short ladder to the deck of the ship. There was sailors all around her climbing the three masts of the schooner, and scurrying on the deck rolling up ropes . Lisbeth stood on the deck when behind her a booming voice demanded to know why she was top side?

"We're under way? I want to talk to Captain Rob Where is he?" She looked up at a very tall and lanky young man with a kerchief tied over his head and his shirt falling loose from his pants.

"The Captain be at the wheel, Miss." He pointed and Lisbeth saw the Captain legs a stride to brace himself from the swells that dipped the ship up and down. Lisbeth made her way to the big wheel that was taller than she was and watched Captain Rob without speaking as he steered the Schooner toward France.

"Lassie, come closer. I've only a glimpse of you from the edge of my eye. I would see you proper." He said.

Lisbeth did as he asked and came up beside him just as the sun peeked over the horizon, startling her with its beauty against the still black sea. "Oh, my, tis a beautiful sight." She said as she turned to smile up at him.

"That it is. Ye are up early! Couldn't ye sleep?" Captain Rob turned questioning eyes and peered at her face. A faint bruise appeared under both her eyes and he lifted his huge hand and cupped her face to see better. Lisbeth jerked away and stammered.

"I'm fine. I felt the ship moving and decided to see what was happening. When will we be there"?

Captain Rob took his time replying, looking her up and down from her blaze of red gold hair to her green velvet gown with the ivory stomacher. She was fetching and it made his lower loins ache with desire for her. Momentarily speechless he concentrated on the wheel and the rise and fall of the schooner.

"Dunna fash yourself, my dear. I must keep us out in the sea to keep the Lobster-backs from getting suspicious. I be stopping in ports along the way before I swing east toward Calais. There is free trade in France, but all boats leaving England are subject to search and seizure if they have anything that they feel would benefit Bonnie Prince Charles cause. I must appear to be going about my normal business." He smiled at her lighting his rather somber face with a brilliance that caught Lisbeth's breath and she quickly stepped away from him, a quivering in her heart that she had never experienced. Captain Rob's ruggedly muscled body made her throb in places that a Lady prudently ignored during waking hours.

Chapter 5

They did indeed stop at every port. Captain Rob knew everyone and though it was Christmas week, commerce was conducted quickly and efficiently. It was hard to see what was brought aboard except the herd of goats which was an exception. Captain Rob told her that these goats were for his farm in Dornoth.

"Lassie, ye could never find a more perfect place in all the land as my Brindle Hall, I've a thousand acres all the richest loam. My truck garden feeds myself and my fifty tenants and I'm bringing the goats for. milk and cheese for my larder. Almost all of the ewes here are pregnant. I've a pasture full of Merino sheep. Their wool will make warm woolens. If they get the woolen mill running again after the English set it afire on their march across the moors and through our town of Dornoth, we'll get a good price for our wool." Captain Robs chest swelled with pride. His attention was diverted by a wayward ram who tried to escape back down the gangplank. He hurried to intercept the goat and caught him. He turned to Lisbeth and with a sweep of his hat bowed.

Captain Rob smiled at Lisbeth. A chill wind ruffled his hair as he moved over a bit so Lisbeth could join him at the wheel. As she inched close to him, his body burned with the desire to have her. A frown appeared on his face as he struggled to control the deep ache in his loins that Lisbeth's innocent presence brought to his body. In his mind he cursed Jerome McIntosh for bringing his family on this fool's errand. Captain Rob didn't even know why he had said yes to this lassie when his good sense screamed NO! In loud urgency. He didn't need the money. The Molly Bee ship's hold was bloated with barrels of gun powder, bales of silk, expensive whiskey, chests full of fine jewelry and countless other treasures all bound for King Louie's Palace.

It had been an extremely lucrative year. There was no better time to spend a few days sailing than to the Palace of Versailles to sell his treasure to King Louie.

However, Captain Fraser's mind drifted beyond the pleasures of an abundant season and focused on his crew with scorn. His crew couldn't wait till they made the port in Calais where they would get their money for this voyage and spend every last piece of eight they had earned on whores and spirits.

Fraser saved his money for a greater purpose. He would soon have enough money to retire to his home at

Brindle Hall in the town of Dornoth, Scotland in the Sutherland region. He would restore the long run-down place of his birth to its former glory. He would return, take his rightful place as Laird of the Fraser Clan and bring prosperity and glory back to the tenants on his war ravaged holdings. Only recently his trading and smuggling had brought Brindle Hall out of poverty. Ever since his father Angus Robert Fraser was killed at the 1715 rebellion the month before he was born, Brindle Hall had struggled to stay ahead of the tax man.

Suddenly Rob felt a chilling shiver run through his body. He looked around and chuckled as he addressed his Ma, Lady Eugenia at home in Brindle Hall. "Now Ma, stop peeking. Ye unnerve me with that trick." Lady Eugenia dabbled in the "black arts" and when her son was away would often watch him in her chalice water. Rob considered it harmless fun and often teased her when he came home, letting her know he felt her presence. It was too bad she couldn't see what the fate of Prince Charles would be. Tis would save him a lot of trouble to know for sure which way the wind blew.

Captain Rob was a practical man. He felt that the cause of the Bonnie Prince Charles Stuart to regain the thrones of England and Scotland was doomed. He'd heard that the Prince had had a small victory against the English in Prosene, but the small band of Highlanders he'd recruited couldn't hold out against the mighty British troops for long. Captain Rob, a man who loved his beloved Scotland, couldn't abide a drunken Prince who wanted Scotland for his own ego. No. He would not win, but if he by chance did win, Captain Rob didn't want to alienate the man either. It was a fine line to maintain, but so far Captain Rob, a smuggler and a procurer of fine Scottish whiskey that he sold to the highest bidder was able to remain apolitical, a supplier who went about his business for his own purposes. Yes, Jerome McIntosh was on a Fool's mission. Bringing his daughter and family with him on it caused Captain Rob to seethe inside. Damn it to hell. Captain Rob had only seen Lisbeth for a short time but he wanted her. Damned if he didn't.

Never in his many travels had he set eyes on such a comely woman. She looked like a sea sprint, a mermaid changed to human form. Her fiery red hair and creamy skin enchanted him. His chest swelled to bursting with the want of her. When he beheld Lisbeth McIntosh, he immediately pictured her as his Lady at Brindle Hall, presiding over his home as mistress. His desire for her made his loins ache, and he knew this, his life would not be complete until he possessed her.

Lisbeth saw the gleam in his eye and hurriedly made her exit, stating, "My family is beholden to ye, Captain. I thank you and now I'll leave you to your duties." She bowed her head and escaped back to the cabin.

Chapter 6

Lisbeth was in the cabin dragging Hugh out of bed when she felt a slight bump. She looked out the porthole and saw that they were docked. A sharp jolt of joy made her smile as she grasped Hugh's covers and pulled.

"Up, Up my boy. Come look out the porthole. We're here. We will see Da soon." Hugh threw off the covers and joined Lisbeth at the porthole.

Hugh looked around the cabin, "Where's Ma and Letitia?"

Lisbeth tousled his hair. "They've been up for hours. Hurry Hugh, you'll miss breakfast if you don't. They'll be wanting us off the boat afore noon." Topside the two grimaced. The bright glare and cold crisp air hit them searing their lungs. Lisbeth looked around her in wonder at the ships moored next to the Molly Bee they were cloaked in white with snow solid as the eye could see on the dock. Lisbeth hurried to the mess where her mother was sipping a cup of tea and Letitia had a mug of hot chocolate.

"Lisbeth, my darling, we're here! Letitia and I watched the ship as we came into port. T'was thrilling to see us glide into the berth. Captain Rob did a smooth job of it." Lisbeth smiled back at her mother who looked happy and her cheeks were rosy. Letitia sat quiet with her cocoa and grunted when Lisbeth tried to get her to come and make a snowball.

"You go Lizzy. Tis much too cold for me." Her lips pouted and Lisbeth sighed. Fourteen was such a contrary age.

Finally Lisbeth went out by herself and scooped up a big fresh ball of snow and patted it. She raised back her arm and threw the snowball as hard as she could; it was by luck alone that it reached the back of Captain Rob's neck. He turned sharply and at once saw who the culprit was. Bending down and scooping up a big ball of his own and as she turned to run he threw it with deadly aim catching her at her neck. With a look of distain that would wither a weaker man, Lisbeth primly walked back to join her mother in the galley.

Chapter 7

It was almost noon; Captain Rob was busy seeing to the offloading of the cargo and giving instructions to his crew for the reloading of new cargo. Lisbeth was grateful that he was as caring and diligent with their needs as he was with his cargo.

While the McIntosh's waited in the carriage, Clarise told them what she knew of the City of Calais .

"Ye are looking at an ancient city that dates from the Roman era when it was known as Caletum." Clarise laughed when Hugh sighed as she prepared to give them a history lesson. "It was part of a Dutch speaking area of France and was known as Kales during the middle ages. Tis the last exit point of France and the first northern entry point from the viewpoint of England, it was a fishing village in the 10th century. By the 13th century in 1224, it was fortified by the Count of Boulogne." Hugh's eyes rolled in his head and he started to whine.

"Ma, enough! What do I care about this dirty, old town." Hugh sulked and stared out of the carriage window at the edge of the dock and watched the pelican that was eating and catching small pieces of fish that a small boy was throwing to him. The bird wore a thick leather collar to keep him from eating the big fish he was trained to hunt. Hugh and Letitia climbed down from the carriage to get a closer look at the bird.

Clarise turned from the sight and reached out to Lisbeth, hugging her tightly to her. "Oh Lisbeth, I wish the Captain would hurry. I'm so eager to see your Da. "Clarise looked up just in time to see Captain Rob coming down the gangplank toward them. "Here he is now. Letitia, Hugh, come, come, we are leaving." Clarise and Lisbeth greeted the Captain with eager smiles.

"Tis a fine day Captain Rob, are we ready to leave"? "Yes, Madame McIntosh. Here's the driver now." The horses stomped their feet impatiently as the driver climbed into the front seat. Captain Rob whistled for Hugh and Letitia who had disregarded their sister's pleading. They came at a run. Captain Rob swung his leg up on the carriage wheel and took his seat next to the driver.

Chapter 8

The carriage lurched along the snow draped roads as the four horses picked their way over the icy ruts churning the road to freezing mud as they drove along. They left Calais far behind them. At dusk they stopped at the Horse and Arms tavern where Captain Rob found two rooms for them.

It was warm by the fire and the tavern had a dining area in the back for the guests with their own small fireplace. Lisbeth and her mother sighed with relief at finally being able to stop for the night. The wench who brought their food was cheerful setting thick bowls of hot onion soup in front of them with the classic chunk of bread and cheese. This was followed by a plate of roasted ham with potatoes and cranberry sauce, probably leftover fare from the Christmas dinner. It was delicious.

"Just think tomorrow we will see your Da!" Clarise smiled at her children and got up, left the table and led them to their room where they were soon asleep.

The little family slept soundly even with the noise of the tavern patrons laughing far into the night. The next morning they barely had time for a cup of hot tea and a scone before Captain Rob was escorting them to the carriage and out again in the grim cold. Rob threw a bear skin rug over their legs and brought hot stones from the inn's fireplace. Placed at their feet the welcome heat of the stones soon warmed them and made the trip more bearable. The driver lashed his whip across the horse's backs barely touching them. They were off.

Chapter 9

It was late afternoon when little party stopped at a wayside inn for tea and a hearty meal of meat pie and ale. Then back in the coach again and the endless road. They sighed with relief when they saw the castle in front of them glowing in the twilight as they turned onto the road that lead through the village of Versailles.

Versailles at dusk was a cozy village and Lisbeth envied the families snug behind their glowing windows catching a peek as the coach continued through town without stopping; straight to the palace.

The Court of Versailles was the center of political power in France. The little family looked in awe at the beautiful palace and marveled that they would be living there with their Da and King Louis XV and his family. There would be children to play with and the court life would be interesting.

The group was un-ceremoniously deposited at the servant's entrance and met at the door by a large woman who spoke in French. Captain Rob asked her in French to find Monsieur Jerome McIntosh and she shook her head. The gist of the conversation was that Monsieur Jerome was with the king and could not be disturbed. She was to take them to their apartments and he would come when he could.

A solemn group followed the portly woman, her bottom jiggling as she swayed in a graceful walk. They were followed by Captain Rob and the driver as well as two footmen who were carrying their luggage. They were taken through long corridors and up wide staircases. Later they were to learn there were over sixty seven staircases in the palace and two thousand plus rooms. The apartment they were given consisted of a big drawing room with tall ceilings and a small breakfast room as well as three bedrooms and a very smelly commode.

As the family settled in and inspected the apartment, Clarise waited impatiently for Jerome. Finally the door swung open and Jerome swept into the room dressed in a silk waistcoat and silver buckles on his shoes. Jerome pushed his wavy brown hair back from his forehead, overcome with emotion at the sight of his family. All he could do was open his arms, tears streaming from his eyes and embrace them.

"Oh my precious ones your safe. Thank God! Thank God!" Clarise, Lisbeth, Hugh, and Letitia crowded around him. Jerome was a mighty man in breadth and yet he stood only an inch or two taller than Clarise and with his pincer glasses and his hair long to his collar he resembled the noted Ben Franklin, a frequent visitor to the palace as an Ambassador from the New American Colonies and a close friend of King Louis.

"My dear children, Rob, thank the Lord you are here and safe." Jerome embraced Clarise and kissed her soundly. He shook Rob's hand and thanked him for bringing them.

"We must have some refreshment." Jerome moved to the bell rope and summoned a very dignified gentleman who spoke to him in French. Jerome rattled off his request in perfect French, astounding Lisbeth who had never heard him speak the language before.

"Now my loves while we wait for our tea tell me how you fare." There was a clamor of noise as everyone tried to talk at once. Finally Jerome raised his hands for quiet and asked each one in turn, starting with the children.

Hugh had just finished telling him of the pelican he had seen when a discreet knock on the door announced their tea. The man rolled in a cart filled with pastries of all kinds and tiny water crest sandwiches as well as tarts and a hot steaming teapot full of tea. The children filled their plates and soon all was quiet as they slurped their tea and munched on the pastries. Jerome and Clarise sat close together with Jerome's arm firmly around her waist.

"Oh my dear I've missed you so much and the children too of course." He looked up and turned to Captain Rob. "My friend, I'm in your debt. We are so grateful to be together and safe. After tea you and I will talk and tell me all that is happening."

"With pleasure Jerome, I've much to tell ye and I'm afraid tis not good," replied Rob seriously.

Chapter 10

The children had finished their tea and were eager to explore. Jerome rang for an English speaking servant who was happy to take them for a tour of the palace. Lisbeth went along too.

They seemed to walk for ages down several staircases to the main rooms and Jerome stopped at a very tall door which opened to a huge room full of mirrors huge with large gold frames.

The kindly old servant bent with age led the way, her skirts swishing. Smiled broadly and launched into a history of the room.

"This is the famous Hall of Mirrors. When young King Louis came back to the palace in 1722 he was only twelve years of age. He was so happy to come back that he rushed out into the gardens where, in spite of the June heat he made the round of all the groves, with his entourage struggling to keep up with him. He then visited all the grand apartments. When he got to this room, the Hall of Mirrors, he lay down on the parquet floor to admire the vault of Le Brun relating to the heroic deeds of his great – grandfather.

The Court imitated him and lay down on the floor beside him. Can you imagine it?" The woman laughed as Hugh lay down and looked straight up at the paintings on the ceiling and exclaimed in wonder.

"Lisbeth, Letitia come and look tis so beautiful." Hugh whispered. Lisbeth and Letitia both laughing at the small boy joined him on the parquet floor and gazed up to the ceiling, right along with him.

Chapter 11

Lisbeth had left the others at the hall of mirrors and made her way to the gardens. She reached the terrace overlooking the formal gardens of the palace and caught her breath. They were beautiful in the late afternoon. The sun was casting long shadows over the rows of formal meticulous topiaries and Lisbeth was stunned at their beauty as she made her way into the garden.

Captain Rob, his report to Jerome concluded, watched her from the window and waited until she had walked far into the garden and stopped in front of the Bassin de Neptune. Then he quietly left the palace and walked toward her. It was dusk by the time he reached her. The silver blue water in the fountain reflected the last rays of sun light. Captain Rob bowed to Lisbeth and kissed her hand, lingering a little longer than was necessary over it.

"Have you and my father made any decisions on when you will be meeting Prince Charles?" Lisbeth trailed her fingers in the fountain as Captain Rob moved close behind her.

"Yes, we leave tomorrow at dawn. Your father must gather the clans and that will take a month or more. The Bonnie Prince is heading toward Inverness and hopes to have a large gathering of the clans before mid- April. It will be a huge gathering of Highlanders .

I'll be taking your father as far as Inverness where he will meet up with the Prince. I will then go to my estate at Brindle Hall and deliver the goats. I will make myself useful to the Prince ferrying men to Inverness for a meeting in early April." Captain Rob saw the look of alarm on Lisbeth's face and squeezed her hand as she moved backwards away from him so she could see his face. He was so tall .

"What of my Ma and my sister, brother, and I, where will we be?" She asked looking frightened, her face flushed bright red with emotion and her huge green eyes looked straight up into his. She was not a child, she would know what was happening.

"All of you will stay here as guests of King Louie until this is all over. Your father has arranged for a fortnight stay in the apartment assigned to him. Your mother will be useful here. One of the servants is in labor. Your mother has already gone to be mid-wife to her."

Lisbeth turned away from him and clutched the side of the Basin of Neptune. Her knuckles turned white as she gripped the edge of the fountain bowl.

"I won't stay here. I'm one and twenty and I know my own mind. I'll go with you and Da." She turned and looked at him defiantly with her chin up. Captain Rob looked at her with dismay.

"War is not for women, my dear." he said softly. "Stay with your Mama. She needs you here." He reached up and grabbed both her arms and hugged her to his chest. "I wouldn't want you in harm's way." He lifted her chin and before she could move away he kissed her square on her lips. Though flustered by the kiss Lisbeth would not be swayed. She wiped her mouth and doubled her fists and in a strength surprising for her size Lisbeth pushed away from him almost losing her balance as she shouted, "No, I'm going with you and Da. I can be of help. I know all my Ma knows of caring for wounds and sickness. I'll come as the ship's physician. You don't have to worry. I can take care of myself. My Da taught me to shoot and I have my own pistol as well." The more Captain Rob tried to dissuade her the more insistent she became.

"I saw that you didn't have a physician with you on the ship. Ma and I had to help your crew with cuts and ailments. I know that you need me." Lisbeth turned and ran for the apartment. She knew she was right. She knew her Da needed her, and as stubborn as Captain Rob was, she knew he needed someone who could help when a sailor was injured.

Chapter 12

Lisbeth slowed to a dignified walk as she opened the door to the apartments and found her parents sitting at the small table in the breakfast room with their tea. Her mother was back from examining the servant who had hours of labor ahead of her.

Her Da looked up as Lisbeth walked into the room. Something in her demeanor alerted him and he stood as if to challenge her.

"Lisbeth, what is it? What's happening?" He went to her and held her gently in his arms as she braced herself to fight.

"Da, I'm coming with you tomorrow." Her mother looked at her in shock and started to protest but Lisbeth raised her hand for silence and her mother held her tongue.

"Listen to me please. I'm one and twenty and I can be useful. I can tend the wounded and help with the sick ones. "Ma. You taught me well and I don't want Da to go alone. Someone must be with him. I'd never forgive myself if he was injured and no one to be there for him. Da, I've already told Captain Rob and he is without a physician on his schooner. Even he knows I'm right. If he is sailing to Inverness and bringing the men to war and hopefully back again he knows he is going to need someone who heals. "

"Ma Ma, I will be very careful and you needn't worry. I'm a woman now and I must go."

After much discussion and pleading with Lisbeth her parents saw her resolve and they resigned themselves to her will. Instead of arguing with her Ma stood up and hugged her. Then the two went to choose herbs and ointments and linens for bandages as well as packing her boxes. The palace kitchen was raided for herbs, garlic, loafs of bread and fresh lemons and oranges. Crates and crates of meats eggs and sides of bacon were sent to the wagons.

Chapter 13

At dawn, Lisbeth was dressed and ready, drinking hot tea and nibbling on a biscuit when Captain Rob came to tell them the carriage and wagons of provisions were waiting. The little group said their goodbyes at the Portico. Ma and Hugh and Letitia wide eyed with tears flowing freely as Lisbeth set off with her Da and Captain Rob. Lisbeth could scarce suppress her excitement. She had stood her ground and won the right to live her life as she chose. Now as the carriage rocked and Da and Captain Rob dozed their heads nodding back and forth to the rhythm of the carriage, Lisbeth began to question herself. Was she a fool? She shook off all doubt with determination and she watched the sun come up from the dark of pre- dawn to the red orb. Finally after two days on the road and another night at the inn they reached the dock where the Molly Bee stood moored late the next day.

Chapter 14

There was a frantic bustle of activity around the schooner as the Captain stepped on board and issued orders as his boots made loud clunks on the deck. Lisbeth and her Da walking quickly behind him.

The Boatswain mate hurried alongside him as he stormed along in his heavy boots. Old Harry would be in charge of the supplies and he wasted not a minute ordering the wagons unloaded and the provisions stowed. "Look sharp men, get these goods below and hurry it up we be off at the tide." He huffed and glared at the men, his steel gray eyes boring into them. His barked orders caused them to quicken their steps and run with their arms loaded and disappearing into the hold as fast as they could move.

Lisbeth was shown to the ship's physician's cabin, much smaller than the Captain's, that would serve as both her bedroom and the sick bay. She busied herself unpacking her clothing and hanging what dresses she had in a small wardrobe built into the side of the ship. The men stomped in with her cases and medical supplies. She had jars, bottles, and the alcohol she put under lock and key.

It would not be used for drinking but to help sterilize wounds. The one hundred proof gin was precious. She knew it would be the only disinfectant she would have. Her Ma had packed an entire case of garlic to be used to help with festering wounds. As bad as it smelled Lisbeth had seen her mother use it as a poultice along with very moldy bread on a young man who had cut his leg which had festered badly. She was amazed when her mother took off the poultice to see the wound healed with no sign of festering. The clean linen she put in a canvas bag to rip into bandages.

"Miss, where do you want me to put your carpetbag?" William peeked shyly in the doorway and looked around at the now fully stocked surgery.

"Oh, thank ye William! Ye can just leave it by the door. I'm going to go get something to eat and tend to it later". She smiled at the young man . William was little more than one and twenty but he had seen much of the world on the Molly Bee. Lisbeth wondered why he chose a life as a seaman and vowed to ask him when she could.

Chapter 15

Hours later she realized that she was exhausted. After surveying her well provisioned cupboards she closed the door. The light lunch she had eaten when William had brought her bag to her cabin was hours ago and her stomach growled as she headed toward the ship's galley .

Lisbeth had been so busy she hadn't noticed the schooner had left the harbor. It had sailed through the channel between England and France and was heading out to the open sea before it turning north toward Scotland. Lisbeth paused a moment to feel the ship's movement.

The three masts groaned as the large sails filled with the wind and the schooners headsail ballooned out past the bowsprit. She had a shallow draft which allowed her to remain in shallow coves waiting for her prey, which was why she was a favorite among both pirates and smugglers. The Molly Bee weighed less than one hundred tons and took to the sea like a seasoned sailor. The sun was setting into the horizon as Lisbeth sighed making her way to the galley. Her severe black gown of light wool that her Ma had given her gave her the appearance of a ship's doctor and hid Lisbeth's quaking tremors as she opened the galley door and stepped over the door-jam to sudden quiet as the ships officers and her Da stared up at her.

"Good evening, gentlemen." Lisbeth blushed when all the crew stood and her Da pulled out a chair for her.

Dinner was lively with her Da and Captain Rob toasting each other with foaming drafts of dark ale. The happiness that she saw in her Da's face warmed Lisbeth's heart and she pushed away thoughts of doubt. At last the meal was over and as tired as Lisbeth was she was glad of an excuse to slip down to her cabin. Minutes after pulling the down comforter around her she was lulled to sleep by the gentle rhythm of the ship.

Chapter 16

The little ship moved north and would moor where ever Jerome directed Captain Rob. He would then row ashore and meet with as many Clansmen as he could at the nearest taverns inflaming the men to fever pitch, getting their pledge and asking them to bring others. They were to meet with as many men as they could muster in the forest near Inverness by the first week of April. This was the pattern all the way up the coast until finally the ship turned into the little harbor in the town of Dornoth. Lisbeth and her father weary of the lobbying for men and money for the Bonnie Prince Charles were invited by Captain Rob to come to his Brindle Hall, a short mile from Dornoth. Willie brought the coach out and had the goats herded off the gangplank and down through the town with the coach leading the way. The lead goat was being coached by Willie with morsels of grain to walk to Brindle Hall. It was late afternoon when the motley group arrived at the crest of a hill. Captain Rob rained the horses and showed them far below Brindle Hall, a stately home butting on the edge of the cliff, overlooking the sea. The sun shone on the leaded glass windows casting a reddish glow of the sunset on them. The lights were twinkling on as the weary group drove up to the front of the Hall. The front door opened and a wiry little woman stood there with a lantern held high.

"That you, Robbie?" She asked slowly walking toward the coach. Rob jumped out of the carriage and swung her into his arms planting a smacking kiss on her cheek.

"Put me down this instant, Robbie." His mother's face was red and Robbie obediently put her feet on the ground but held her around the waist as he took her to introduce her to Lisbeth and Jerome.

"Ma, we have guests. This is Jerome McIntosh and his daughter, Lisbeth. This is my mother, Lady Eugenia Fraser."

Eugenia looked sharply at Lisbeth and then at her Da. She suddenly bowed her head and led them into the Hall without preamble.

"I bid ye welcome to Brindle Hall. Willie will show you to your rooms. Dinner will be within the hour." With that Eugenia turned and grabbed Robbie's arm and started to lead him away into the parlor. Robbie dropped his mother's arm and turned to Lisbeth, gathering her close to him. Eugenia covered her surprise with a frown.

"Lisbeth, I hope that you will be very comfortable in my home." He led her into the Hall leaving his mother to follow with Jerome. After showing them their rooms and leaving them to freshen up, Robbie hurried down to the kitchen to tell Hallie that there would be three more for dinner.

"Mister Robbie, your Ma just knew ye would be home today. She pestered me to prepare your favorite meal. I done put a ham to roast with fresh biscuits and gravy. Dinna ye worry none , Hallie made plenty for ye and your guests." Everyone at the Hall knew of Eugenia's dabbling in magic and had come to trust her when she said something was imminent.

Robbie gave Hallie a big squeeze, barely able to surround her ample waist with his long strong arms. He picked a package tied out of his valise and handed it to her. "I got this for ye from Paris, France just as I promised."

"Mister Robbie, what ye got there? Oh my lord, look at that! My goodness I ain't never had a dress so fine. ! thank ye Robbie." With that she hurried out of the room to try on the sea green dress of fine spun cotton.

Chapter 17

The reunion with Rob's Ma and the tenants of Brindle Hall lasted for a week. Rob loved showing off his home to Lisbeth. Eugenia was proper and polite but cool toward Lisbeth, causing Rob to show her even more attention. The first morning after a breakfast of eggs, kippers and toast, Rob took Lisbeth for a tour on horseback of his land. "There are over 1,000 acres and it's all mine all the way up to the seawall. Once I'm free to spend my time here, I'm going to plow and plant. The new goats will bring fresh lineage." Just then Lisbeth's horse screamed and took off with Lisbeth clinging to the saddle horn. Robbie raced behind her trying to stop the horse as it raced straight for the cliff. At the last moment he grabbed Lisbeth from her saddle and veered to the left as Lisbeth's horse plunged over the cliff and onto the rocks below.

"Lisbeth, what happened?" What made Daisy bolt like that? Rob brought Thunder, his Roan to a stop and with shaking legs, Lisbeth slid out of his arms and down to the ground where Rob joined her, holding her tight to him till she stopped shaking.

"I'm all right, poor Daisy". Lisbeth buried her head in Rob's shirt and sobbed. Rob comforted her and reached under her chin and lifted her face to his gently kissing her sweet mouth. "Oh Lisbeth tis frightened to death I be."

Lisbeth shuddered and wiped the tears from her eyes, straightened her dress and sighed. I've never had a horse shy and run like that. What could have happened? Do you have bees?" The two looked around to see if there were any insects nearby. Rob then helped her up and she rode behind him back to the Hall.

In the attic Eugenia watched in her chalice and when she saw that Lisbeth was safe she clinched her fists and pounded them on the table. "Damn her, I'll get her yet!" Eugenia took a bit of the lace she had snipped off of Jerome's cuffs and a snip off the blue ribbon that Lisbeth had left on her dresser that morning and dropped them into a candle. Watching them burn to ash she chanted their names and evoked her black art to destroy them both.

Chapter 18

Lisbeth and Rob dismounted back at the stables. Rob attempting to calm her down, speaking in a soothing voice led her to the edge of the fields where next spring crops would be grown, continued to tell her about his plans for Brindle Hall, hoping to quell her fear with normal bantering.

"I'm going to plant potatoes, a new crop that I heard about in Paris. Before we go with your Da, I'm going to show Moses how to plant them, when we get back we will get the rest of the crops in." Rob walked with her to the chicken pen and went in and picked up some eggs from the nesting boxes. The eggs were chocolate brown.

"I've never seen eggs that color before! Can you eat them?" Lisbeth looked at the beautiful clutch of eggs in the straw basket that Rob held. Bravely she chatted with Rob. Only her paleness showing how shook up she was.

"Oh yes. These are my pride". He held up the black chicken with its copper sheen on its' feathers as if they were dipped in gold. "These are Black Copper Marans. I got them in France last year and plan on not only having enough for our needs here at Brindle Hall, but to breed them and sell them at market. They are very unusual. I'm sure that they will cause a lot of interest." Rob grinned as he handed the silky hen to her. She stroked its feathers. They were as soft and slippery as satin. Suddenly Lisbeth frowned and lifted her hand to her head. A blinding headache momentarily blinded her and she cried out in pain.

Rob frowned set his jaw and rushed her back to the Hall. He took her into the kitchen and left her with Hallie who fixed her a cup Chamomile tea. Rob took the stairs two at a time and slammed into her mother's sanctuary catching her over her chalice with a wicked look on her face.

"Woman, you will stop your trifling with the woman I love! This is beyond natural. And if ye don't stop I'll have you burned as a witch myself. Ye trifle with my woman ye are dead to me." With that Rob turned his face, flushed with rage and stalked out of the room leaving his mother with his ultimatum. He hurried back to Lisbeth. It was only then in the warmth of the kitchen that he told Lisbeth about his mother's "arts" and warned her to be on guard against them. Hallie stood behind Lisbeth and marked her with the sign of the cross. From then on

Hallie would pray daily to keep Lisbeth safe and nullify the black magic.

Chapter 19

The next morning Lisbeth was eager to leave fearing and knowing that the incident yesterday was the work of Eugenia. The three said their goodbyes. Eugenia and Lisbeth were cool and wary of each other. Captain and her Da and Lisbeth boarded the Molly Bee and made their way north. They picked up men all along the coast until the ship was bursting. Men were sleeping on the deck and having to take turns to sit in the mess hall for their meals. Lisbeth was kept busy tending to their ills and ailments the men brought with them, from infected toenails to boils on their necks and dropsy.

The Clans stood waiting for the Molly Bee to dock. Small groups of McIntosh's, Grants, Ferguson's, and Murrays as well as Gordon's and Ross in their hunting plaids marched up the gangplank at every harbor they stopped in. The schooner sat low in the water when at last it turned north and straight up to Inverness where it was anchored in a small firth. The men quietly got off and walked into the woods where the Bonnie Prince was waiting for them.

Lisbeth her Da and Captain Rob were the last off the ship. Lisbeth carried a chest of medical supplies and other supplies in the wagon pulled by four horses. Willie drove the team as the Captain and her Da watched the woods for ambush. Jerome turned to his daughter.

"Lisbeth the Prince has sent word for me to meet with him today. I am verra pleased that he thinks so highly of me. Mark my words, we will be dancing in the palace come summer." Her Da's chest swelled in pride. Jerome saw the look of worry clouding his daughter's eyes.

"Dinna worry, my dear, this rising will be over soon, with the Prince leading us. I'd trust him with my life by God."

Chapter 20

They arrived at the edge of the encampment and Jerome asked to be taken to Prince Charles, tent straight away.

The Scottish camp sprawled for miles it seemed. Lisbeth followed her father and Captain Rob past hundreds of tents and cook fires where dusk turned the banners an anonymous gray. A Peregrine falcon his eye on dinner swooped down upon a fleeing lark, sending a chill of doom along Lisbeth's spine.

The three reined up in front of a pavilion where Bonnie Prince Charles camped. From inside the tent voices rose in a bawdy song and loud laughter. The strong smell of whiskey wafted out of the tent as Captain Rob and her father gingerly poked their heads inside.

The Prince looked up as Jerome entered. "Jerome McIntosh Sire, Commander of the MacKintosh clan. Jerome dropped to one knee and showed a leg. Captain Rob bent his knee and Lisbeth curtsied in homage to the little Prince, who had a whiskey decanter in one hand and a just filled goblet in the other. The great gold and crimson lion banner of the exiled King James of the Scots was draped behind his chair. The Prince's servants had softened the ground with rushes mixed with Rosemary to sweeten the dusty air. The Prince raised his silver cup to his lips and drank before he spoke.

"How many Lobster-backs will we have to fight?" Prince Charles asked as he poured drinks for them all.

Jerome stood straight in front of the prince. "Five thousand, the English are a day's march from Culloden. From all the reports that's where they will make their stand," Jerome blustered as he tipped his drink and emptied it wiping his mouth with the back of his hand.

The Prince finished off his drink and threw the cup onto the rushes and snarled. "We will meet them at Culloden. We'll break camp and leave immediately. If we march all night we will with God's help be there ahead of them."

Jerome stammered, "I saw no sign of English outriders, but surely General Cumberland must know we'll try to cut them off. If we march the men with no time to rest they will be exhausted!"

The Prince stood up and his face a beet- red stammered. "Strike the tents now I say, we leave immediately. " The Prince turned to his page, "Get my sword and saddle my horse".

Jerome bowed his head. "My sword is yours, always my Lord."

The prince lifted Jerome's head and looked deep into his eyes.

"The men will see my confidence in all of my commanders, including your good self, and know it's my confidence in ye that allows me to drive the men so hard through this dark night. Now leave me."

Jerome turned and left the tent with Lisbeth and Captain Rob solidly behind him.

Chapter 21

All through the camp the orders to strike their tent could be heard and sparks flew as the men stomped out the fires with their feet. Horses were saddled and wagons loaded. The men silently marched through the night north toward Culloden.

Lisbeth wrapped in her cloak rode beside her father and the Captain following the long line of men through the craggy pass and on to Culloden. They marched through the black night silent as possible with only the trudge of their feet and the soft blowing of the horses and arrived at Culloden as wisps of fog drifted from gray to gold in the fresh morning light.

They set up a rough camp and sat eating beef jerky and cold oat cakes washing them down with the cold water of the burn. Heavy fog shrouded the camp. The troops grouped together by clan, Frasers, Mackintosh's, MacDonald's and Fergusons, Grants, Gordon's and Murray's and Ross's. Jerome left Lisbeth safe in the shadow of the birches with Captain Rob to guard her and went to where the Clan Mackintosh hunkered down a half mile away. Jerome's clansmen had more bravado than fight training and the troops were in a writhing mass of disorder. They were eager for glory but green as a spring meadow. Jerome motioned for silence and ordered his commander to bring the troops to attention. The ragged group in their red and green plaids wrapped around them for warmth struggled to their feet, adjusted their kilts and looked up at Jerome. He addressed the men and saw their backbones rise up to the challenge he threw at them. Just then the sound of an English trumpet sounded and was answered by another and another. The English were coming and as the bagpipes whined Jerome rode to the front of his clan. In moments a huge swarm of Scotsman were formed into a fighting unit, turned toward the battlefield in-mass.

"A Moray! A Moray! For Scotland and King James!" Jerome screamed, bent over his horse and kicked it into a canter. Sword raised he led his men out on to the battlefield.

Driving rain and sleet blew the fog away. The icy sleet from the northeast drove needles of ice into the faces of the exhausted Jacobite army. Grimly they raised their swords and axes and ran behind Jerome.

The troops faced each other on the moor and moved steadily forward. When they were still a hundred yards from Cumberland's right, the English's orders were given to "Make ready....present.... fire!" About one third of the Ross's fell, either dead, dying or severely wounded.

Three times the Jacobite's made to advance in the hope of enticing the Redcoats to break formation and attack, and three times they failed. The line held steady and the MacDonald's died. It was too much and they fell back in disarray. Panic became widespread, the tartan tide flooded away from the killing place. The ceasefire was ordered in the Hanoverian ranks. What lay in front of them were heaps of dead and dying where the fighting and gunfire had been most effective. The Bonnie Prince had gone: he left his supporters to their individual fates and made his escape. His commander of Prince Charles' Life Guards shouted after him as he departed, "Run, you cowardly Italian!" Lord George Murray still remained; his aides, thinking he might make a solo charge took hold of his bridle and led him from the field in tears."

The royal dragoons seemed to have been given free rein. Without any kind of order they scoured the positions previously held by the Highlanders. Swords slashing anybody that moved. The infantry was ordered to advance in line to officially take and occupy their enemy's positions, using their bayonets to seal off any wounded highlanders unable to make an escape. The battle was over.

Lisbeth watched with horror as her father and his clansmen were wounded in front of her. She lost sight of her father for a moment. Then she saw him being dragged off the field alive but surrounded by the Lobsterbacks. She ran out of the trees heading for him when Captain Rob grabbed her from behind and held her tight to him as he soothed her and carried her back to the safety of the trees.

"Come now, dinna weep, dear one. We can't help him now. Later we'll see where they take him and then we'll do what we can." He helped her on to her horse and the two stole off into the trees. They reached their wagon and Willie quickly helped Lisbeth aboard. She sobbed and collapsed as she thought about her father and all of the young Clansmen who had gone into that battle ignorant of war and green as toads.

Rob, held Lisbeth in his arms as they headed back to Inverness and the Molly Bee. They had entered a trail just wide enough for their wagon when Lisbeth looked over her shoulder and screamed! The tents of the Scots were set on fire and a fire storm of leaping flames was licking toward them as the fire gained momentum. Robbie looked back and behind them trees burst into flames sending sparks cascading over the wagon and horses. Rob beat out the sparks as they landed and hollered to William! "Go! go faster! The fire is gaining on us!"

William lashed the horses and wild eyed they sped over the ground barely missing trees and branches in their way. At last their wild ride was over. William brought the horses to a stop. The wagon and horses were led up the gangplank and safely aboard. Captain Rob yelled, "Set sail." The men hastened to obey and sails billowed as the schooner was launched before the English could close off the harbor. They arrived at the secret cove at dusk the next evening.

Chapter 22

Lisbeth finished binding the last wound, quickly locked the door to her surgery as the small band of refugees spilled off the schooner and melted into the forest heading for their homes, hoping to not meet the English before they were safely home and hidden in their Crofts.

William had a saber wound on his right thigh that Lisbeth had cleaned and stitched. She gave him a dose of whiskey to help with the pain. applying crushed garlic and moldy bread she made a poultice, like her mother had taught her and wrapped William's thigh in a soft clean cloth and sent him to his hammock to rest. The rest of the men she treated the same way. It was a patched up and whiskey soaked crew that helped Captain Rob guide the Molly Bee out of the cove and through the harbor in the dark moonless night. They reached the North Sea and the Molly Bee cut across the water out of harm's way. The Molly Bee and her crew would be fugitives and the English would stop at nothing to capture them if they could find them. Captain Rob wasn't going to let them find them. They headed for France and once again Lisbeth found herself in Calais. Before entering the harbor a crewman who was handy with a paint brush brushed out the "M" in the Molly Bee and substituted a "P" turning it into the Polly Bee. The paint was barely dry when the schooner slid into its berth in Calais harbor.

The exhausted crew and Lisbeth slept; Relief of their safe arrival allowed them the first worry free sleep in days. It was then in the quiet of her cabin that Lisbeth was able to grieve for her father and say a prayer for his safety. Rob reassured her that they would probably take him to the tower and they would try to negotiate for his release. Rob had sent word to his solicitor in England by way of the ship Horn Blower. It was all that could be done for now.

At the short, quiet knock on the cabin door Lisbeth opened it and Rob stepped inside. Lisbeth burst into tears and Rob gathered her into his arms.

"Dinna fash, my Lovely, ye are right to grieve your Da. I willna' promise you that he can be saved, but I do promise ye that I will try." He moved her gently toward the bed and pulled down the covers. Lisbeth looked up at him with huge eyes as he tucked her into bed. He smiled and assured her.

"I'll not take advantage of your grief. When you come to me I want it to be in joy. We will wait." He hushed her protests and kissed her full, soft mouth, stood up with a sigh, turned down the lantern, and quietly left her. Lisbeth yearned for him and yet she respected him. Yes, later, in joy they would join, she knew it and blissfully fell into a dreamless sleep.

It was late; though the cabin was still dark, a slice of sunlight streamed through a crack in the curtain. It was chilly, but warm and cozy under the quilts, Lisbeth thinking of Rob as she struggled awake. Suddenly a stab of grief slammed into her as her mind brutally recalled the massacre and her father's capture. Lisbeth scrambled out of bed and hurried into her clothes.

Chapter 23

After a quick breakfast of coffee and oatcakes with honey, Rob had three horses saddled and walked them off the gangway onto the dock. Lisbeth barely had time to grab her cloak and a small valise with necessities in it. Quickly they were off to the Abbey where Rob's friend, Mother Superior Agnes Scarholt a Norwegian transplant to France, now held court. They would leave William in the good hands of the Mother Superior to heal. The Abbey was off the road, beyond the forest secluded and serene in a small clearing. There was a wall around the Abbey where the Monks tended a kitchen garden. Behind the long low building there was a shed for their horses. Rob helped Lisbeth down and handed the reins to the small thin stable boy and ordered fresh water and grain for the horses. Then he turned to William.

"If I help ye, can ye walk?" Rob asked.

William nodded and grimaced when Rob grabbed him around the waist. "Lean on me Willie, I'll take your weight. Come Lisbeth, Agnes looks worried. I've much to tell her".

Rob tenderly guided Lisbeth to the heavy plank door where the Mother Superior Agnes waited.

Lisbeth collapsed sobbing into her arm's, Mother Superior put her arms around her and led her inside.

"There, there, I'm sorry for your grief. Come with me. I'll ring for tea. We'll have it in my study and you can tell me all about it." Lisbeth felt safe and allowed herself to be coaxed into a small warm room, its walls lined with bookshelves and a blazing fire roaring in the hearth.

The Tea arrived with a liberal lacing of sugar and a shot of brandy.

"Thank ye, Mother. It was so horrible when my Da was taken prisoner. I dinna see if he was injured, but I couldn't go to him and I must. My Da needs me." Lisbeth began to sob into her hands. Rob reached into his pocket and produced a large white clean kerchief.

"Here, my Leamenn. Wipe your eyes. We will gather our strength here with my dear friend Agnes and then tomorrow we will be home with your Ma."

The next day, Lisbeth and Rob bid goodbye to William and the good Mother Superior and headed for Versailles. It was another day's journey. The riders were exhausted when they saw the gleam of the palace lit against the night. Leaving their horses in the stables Rob and Lisbeth were immediately taken to Lisbeth's mother, Clarise. Lisbeth opened the door and fell into her mother's arms.

"Oh Ma, Da has been captured!" Clarise broke into tears and Rob led the two hysterical women into the parlor. He gently guided the two crying women to chairs around the fireplace. He asked Clarise where Hugh and Letitia were. I want them to hear what has happened to their Da."

"It was a nightmare! Your Da and all of the others didn't have a chance. But I promise ye we will do all we can for your Da. Rob stopped and drank deeply of the dark rum in his cup. He'd try his best, but his heart was heavy with foreboding.

Letitia and Hugh began to wail. Lisbeth and Clarise hugged them and soothed their tears.

Clarise seemed to gain strength and resolve. Holding her children close to her she promised them,

"I will go see your Da and will do all I can for him. I assure you. Now children we must rest and be ready to leave at first light." She turned and led Hugh and Letitia to their beds.

Lisbeth talked urgently to Rob, and inquired.

"What will happen at the trial?" She looked up at Rob with her big green eyes pleading with him to save her father.

Rob crushed her to him. "I promised ye I will do all I can to help him. But I warn ye tis bad trouble he is in, my Leamenn ."

The sun had just tipped over the horizon when the coach started out down the road toward Calais. Rob was riding his horse, leading hers. Lisbeth wished he was inside with them. They traveled all day and by nightfall after a bowl of hot Scotch's Broth and bread at a roadside inn, they decided to press on. It was midnight when they arrived in Calais and the coach stopped on the dock.

Captain Rob led them to the Polly Bee hidden by the foggy night. Rob roused the crew and the schooner slipped out of the harbor bound for England.

They were two days on the water again, stopping in small ports buying and selling goods to the locals to resell on market days. The journey seemed to take forever. Lisbeth walked the deck and willed the ship to be off again. Rob found her by the bow. Lisbeth allowed him to hold her tight and shared her worries with him.

"Oh Rob, all I can think of is that my Da is scared. I'm so frightened for him. "Lisbeth turned and pressed her body against his chest.

"I know, Leamenn, ye must be brave. Your mother will be allowed to see him. I've a friend in the jailer who will take a small package of Laudanum she can take to give him to calm him if they find him guilty."

We must trust that whatever is to happen your Da will not suffer. This I can promise ye. As for the rest, I do not know."

The two held each other tightly taking comfort as they could. There was no knowing what would happen now.

Chapter 24

The trial was the day after they made port. Lisbeth, Clarise and Rob attended it leaving Hugh and Letitia at the London house with George Crane, the caretaker watching it for them. The house had not been vandalized, thanks to George, who kept up the appearance of occupancy with lighted lamps in the windows and the garden neatly tended.

It was with a sad heart that they watched as Jerome was led into the Dock in front of the magistrate and promptly found guilty and sentenced to immediate execution by beheading. The shocked trio made their way back to the house. They gently told Letitia and Hugh who cried throughout the night, until finally falling into a fretful sleep.

The next morning the sad group went to the prison for a final goodbye with their Da.

The gates to the tower swung open and Clarise and Lisbeth, Letitia and Hugh were bid enter and led to a cold dank cell. Their Da was haggard and looked so old, withdrawn into himself. He barely saw them. But quickly realized who they were and opened his arms. They all moved into them. All tried to be brave but the sniffling gave them away.

"My dear one's I'm so sorry. I was a fool to be fooled by Prince Charles, he was a coward." he halted struggling to find words as Clarise put a finger to his lips and kissed him. No words were necessary.

The bones of Jerome's face were pronounced. His eye sockets set so deep that his eyes were sunken and hidden from them. The family's love for him comforted him. They in turn were comforted by his soft assurances that he would see them again when they were all gathered together in heaven. Lisbeth choked back her tears as she kissed her Da a final goodbye and was led out of the cell. They left their mother for a moment alone with her husband.

Chapter 25

The drums were beating loud and slow, moving pace of the men in chains being brought to the scaffold in a cart, up Tower Hill near the Tower of London where they had been held since being captured. Lisbeth clung to her mother.

Jerome McIntosh had been tried for the crime of high treason to the King of England. He would pay with his life at the henchmen's axe .

The cart carrying the prisoners drew to a halt in front of the scaffold and five men, her father among them began their last journey. The men were blindfolded and Lisbeth craned her neck to see her father the next to the last prisoner as he was led to the top of the platform. Even though such a horror awaited him, Lisbeth couldn't turn away. She had to watch and memorize the last movements of her father as he calmly waited his turn. The drums were louder as the first prisoner was led to the block and his neck stripped bare to assure a clean chop, the next two followed swiftly, the thud of the axe echoed loudly through the silent, stunned crowd. Lisbeth prayed that her father had taken the Laudanum and was unaware of the proceedings around him. They had paid with all of the gold they had on them that the jailer would give him the sedative before this last journey.

The crowd grew quiet as the jailer walked to the front of the scaffold and announced that Jerome McIntosh was to be executed by beheading for the crime of treason against the Crown. This caused the crowd to go wild and a shout went up from the stands.

Jerome was led to the block and his neck bared. The drums started up as the executioner nodded and in one clean sweep of the axe her father was no more. Lisbeth closed her eyes as the drums stopped and heard the thud of the axe as it came down. As one, Lisbeth, and her mother, swooned in a dead faint.

Robbie stood rooted to the spot unable to help Lisbeth and her family as he recognized the last man to mount the stairs to the scaffold. Robbie blanched when he realized it was his grandfather, Simon, the Fox Fraser, the mighty Chieftain of the Fraser Clan himself and 11th Earl of Lovat. Robbie moved closer and caught the old Foxe's eye. Simon nodded to him and winked. Then to Robbie's surprise Simon bantering to the crowd.

"You'll get that nasty head of yours chopped off you ugly old Scotch dog," cried the old woman in the London street. Simon retorted, "I believe I shall, you old English bitch." Just then the viewing stand collapsed killing several spectators and causing chaos and shouting from trapped spectators. The old Fox surveyed the mess and shouted back at them.

"The more mischief, the better sport." He then turned to the executioner and smiled at him with a merry twinkle in his eye. He tested the axe's edge and told his friends to cheer up since, he, after all was cheerful. Joking with the executioner about how he would be angry if the man didn't make a neat job of it, he finally laid his head on the block without a tremor.

When the axe went down in a clean accurate kill, Robbie turned and heaved, wiping his mouth with his sleeve. He knelt down to Lisbeth and her family, helping them up and moving them away from the scene.

Chapter 26

Robbie guided Lisbeth and her family to the carriage waiting in the alley. Lisbeth laid her head against the carriage seat and stared straight ahead so deep in shock that Robbie couldn't rouse her. When they reached the Polly Bee, Robbie carried her to his cabin.

Captain Rob gave orders to cast off immediately and the Polly Bee left the dock under one sail just enough to move the ship out to sea.

Lisbeth woke with a start and finding herself in Rob's bed and the ship moving she hastened to return to her cabin and joined her sister in the top bunk. Hugh was in a trundle below blissfully a sleep.

When the schooner hit a wave that caused the little ship to wallow it woke Lisbeth and she struggled to her feet. She felt around her until her hand touched the lightweight velvet of her gown, the gown she had worn to her father's execution. No matter now what she wore, she struggled into it and pulled the soft wool cape around her as she stepped out of the cabin.

Once out on the deck Lisbeth was struck by the darkness of the night and the huge array of stars above her, off to starboard was just a slit of a moon lighting their way. The deck was empty of sailors and only one lone man stood at the wheel. As Lisbeth walked toward him she couldn't mistake the tall slim body. Captain Rob stood with his legs braced against the rolling of the ship. Its bow pointed toward Scotland and turned as Lisbeth came up beside him.

"Well, my dear ye've awakened! I ordered the cook to leave a pot of soup on the back of the stove for ye and your family if ye think ye could eat a bit?"

Lisbeth shook her head, brushed past him and ran to the front of the ship. The waves were breaking over the bow and Lisbeth stood braced against the black fury hurdling toward the schooner. She stood defiant, held on to the bow, and shook her fist at the black void in front of her. Behind her captain Rob motioned to his First Mate to take over the wheel. Rob moved quickly to Lisbeth, gathered her in his arms and held on to her as tightly as he could. He carried her back to his cabin with the intention of helping her in her grief and there snug in his big bed, Lisbeth turned to Robbie. Rob only meant to comfort her but suddenly an urgency to possess her overcame his reserve. His mouth was on her, sucking her in with a desperate hunger that threatened to consume them both. He covered her with his massive body, nuzzled her neck and kissed her. Rob's mouth reached her breast. He watched her eyes go dark molten green, lighted by the lantern swaying above them. Quickly he stripped off her dress and not able to stop himself plunged into her with abandon. Lost in the softness of her, he shoved her knees up and thrust deeper inside of her with raw blind want.

Sensations deep inside her erupted. Hot fire smoldered into a deep release, as she went limp, and became sated. The two spooned together and somewhere in the night Captain Rob became Robbie.

Clarise knew as soon as she saw the empty bed. In her grief she hadn't the strength to confront Lisbeth, so she pretended to be asleep when Lisbeth crept back into the cabin. At dawn a ruby red sun, stained the sky.

Chapter 27

The schooner slipped into the harbor below Brindle Hall in the late afternoon. Hurrying to be ready Clarise took water and soap to Hugh's face.

"Ouch, Ma that hurts. I can mind my own face." Hugh turned away from Clarise and scrubbed his face with the wet cloth. Before she could inspect him, he had dashed out the door and ran onto the deck to escape her.

Clarise sighed, but didn't bother chasing him. She was much to shaken with grief and worried about Lisbeth. Clarise looked up as Lisbeth finished dressing.

"Lisbeth, I'm worried for ye. The Captain is a man of the world and no match for a young woman of your innocence. Lisbeth's head snapped up and she looked her mother straight in the eye.

"Ma, I'm not as innocent as ye think. Robbie and I have an understanding." She stopped grabbed the hair brush and savagely brushed her hair. She'd say no more.

The Polly Bee was docking when a cry went up and Lisbeth watched as Hallie came rushing to the dock.

"Captain Rob, Captain Rob. The English were here looking for you. They beat us with a whip. Oh Captain Rob, it was terrible."

Hallie threw her apron over her face and sobbed into it.

Lisbeth followed Rob into the great hall where she saw Eugenia on the stair heading for her lair. Lisbeth turned and started up the stairs behind her. When she got to the attic she opened the door and faced Eugenia just as she was starting to form another spell.

Lisbeth knocked the chalice onto the floor and confronted Eugenia.

"Ye are a horrid old crone and I blame you for my father's death. Ye jealous old fool. I was prepared to love ye like my own Ma, but now I despise ye."

Eugenia backed away from Lisbeth who marched up to her. She reached up to shake her and Eugenia backed blindly toward the open French doors with Lisbeth right behind her, Eugenia backed straight into the railing, toppled over the side and down onto the rocks below.

Lisbeth stood looking down in shock. Slowly she walked out of the attic and down to where her Robbie was.

Chapter 28

The next day Lisbeth opened the door to the ladies chapel. Candles were burning inside. She peeked inside and saw Rob at the bier of his mother only his shaking shoulders told her he was shuddering in grief.

"Oh Rob, I'm so sorry." Lisbeth touched his shoulder and he looked up with tears streaming down his face and shrugged her away from him. He got up and turned his face like stone and walked past Lisbeth and out the door. He shut himself in his room with his Overseer Frank who explained, "My Lord, they came yesterday at breakfast. They lined us all up against the wall and whipped us." Frank drained the whiskey and wiped his mouth on his sleeve. Your Ma stood up to them and they whipped her too!"

Rob stared into the fire then with resolve announced. "We'll bury her tomorrow. Now leave me man." He turned toward the fire lost in his good memories of his Ma before she went to the black arts, gone from him like a whiff of smoke. Frank left him and when he walked into the foyer he saw Lisbeth standing in the hall. She nodded at Frank and walked into Rob's room, shutting the door.

Chapter 29

The morn was brisk and cold as the small group walked behind the casket of Eugenia Fraser to the tiny cemetery. Rob stood, his arm tight around Lisbeth. It only took a few minutes to commend Eugenia to the eternal arms of God . Rob turned away and left the cemetery.

At Brindle Hall, Rob spoke to the mourners I thank ye for coming today. "Ye are welcome in my home. Come in, have drink and food. Ye are a great comfort to me today."

The fire in the great hall burned hot. Lisbeth and her family sat next to Rob as they were served strong spirits and led to a groaning table of sliced ham, a great bowl of mashed potatoes with hot gravy. There was apple pie from the dried apples of summer and pudding.

After the meal Rob was on his feet.

"My friends, today is a sad, sad day for me and yet a hopeful one as well. Today we buried the mistress of Brindle Hall. I ask you now to welcome my lady, Lisbeth McIntosh, as the new mistress. Lisbeth and I are hand-fast." He turned to Lisbeth and went down on one knee. "After the period of mourning is over we will marry." He looked into Lisbeth's eyes and she smiled up at him and nodded.

Robbie took a silver ring with a ruby stone and slid it onto her hand.

Lisbeth and Rob turned to their guests and accepted their congratulations. Suddenly a fiddler struck up a tune and the somber event warmed into a celebration of life with great respect for all they had lost. Robbie and Lisbeth circled the room shaking hands, being hugged all around.

Outside in the new grave there was a tiny shudder disturbing the dirt then all was still.

Book two.

Brindle Hall

April

1747

Chapter 30

The pelican walked along the shore and snatched at the tidbits that Hugh tossed to him. Lisbeth watched her brother Hugh, a wee boy of almost eleven, so sweet and his pet pelican lost in each other and quickly turned away. Ah, to be a small child again and not have the worry of being an adult. Lisbeth sighed. She almost wished it and yet when she remembered her Robbie, Laird of Brindle Hall, remembered his kisses and the mystery of their first joining she couldn't help but rejoice that she was not a lassie any more but fully capable of mating with the man of her dreams. She sighed again and worried her nail. She and Robbie were hand-fast and for all purposes married. But Lisbeth would have a proper wedding with a priest and all of her family and tenants of Brindle Hall there to rejoice with them.

Lisbeth called to her brother, "Hugh, time to feed the chickens and see that ye lock the coop when ye finish!"

Lisbeth turned away from her brother and his feathered companion and walked toward the rugged rocks that hid the cave where Robbie had once stored his whiskey, protected from the raiding English and where he now hid himself. Since the Culloden massacre in the spring of 1746, where the Scottish Highlanders had made their last stand against the English and lost, Robbie was now forced to hide. How long before the King relented and pardoned the survivors of the uprising at Culloden. Lisbeth sighed. It would be a long time and though it was wonderful to have Robbie so close that she could see him every day, she felt he must escape to France where King Louie would protect his old friend. Lisbeth set her face determined that she could convince Robbie that the time had come to take the schooner to France where she knew he would be safe. The last raiding party of Lord Snowdon and his troops completely destroyed the crops and livestock. They would not stop until Robbie gave himself up or disappeared so thoroughly that they would know that he was gone. Lord Snowdon was canny and sensed that Robbie was still near. Lisbeth must get him to see reason. She developed a plan with William, Dupree, Robbie's best friend and first mate on the Polly Bee. They had changed the schooner's name from the Molly Bee to the Polly Bee to avoid the blockade. William had agreed to sail the schooner tonight right up to where Robbie was hiding in the cave that concealed all of the whiskey. All Robbie had to do was agree and step onto the schooner's deck at midnight and they would sail off to safety in France.

Chapter 31

Lisbeth visited Robbie every day and brought him fresh bread, meat and cheese. Sometimes she was able to get fruit on market day in Dornoth. She looked around for the English soldiers and even watched to see that none of her tenants were close by. No one knew Robbie was still at Brindle Hall, not even her family. Only William knew. If no one knew then they were safe from the English. The coast was clear. Lisbeth hurried to the rocky boulder- hidden entrance. She prayed that Robbie would accept their plan and go tonight.

"Robbie, I'm here" she called and out of the shadows he came.

"Oh, my sweet! Ye are a picture for sure me girl!" Robbie was hidden in depths of the cave, only his voice boomed out to her.

"I watched ye come. Come give me a kiss." Robbie moved out of the shadow of the cave and Lisbeth slipped into his arms. Oh, he felt so good. Lisbeth missed him especially at night when the bed seemed so large and her loneliness made her ache for him. She was thankful that she could see him daily but the constant secretiveness was wearing, making her nerves taut and on edge. She sighed as he released her. Robbie noticed the sigh and looked closely at her.

Her gray- green eyes were smudged with dark circles and her long tresses of red- gold seemed lank and washed of their deep auburn color. Lisbeth looked exhausted!

Rob sighed and wiped a hand across his once ruddy complexion, now pasty white from his months in the cave. His eyes still had their sparkle of sea foam green and though he had lost weight in his confinement he was broad of shoulder, tall and lanky. Rob dipped his head close to Lisbeth's and whispered.

"What is it my Love"? He looked deep in her eyes and as much as Lisbeth didn't want to tell him since she knew that he was feeling just as frustrated as she was she finally blurted it out.

"Oh Robbie my love. When will this time of hiding and secrecy be over? What can we do? I want to be a proper wife to ye and this hiding and catching quick snatches of love when we can isn't how I want our life together to be. I want us to live openly and proudly." She sighed again, knotting her fists at her side as she realized that all she was doing was adding to his pain. She couldn't help it. The situation of hiding from the English in order to avoid arrest as a war criminal was wearing on her.

"I don't know me Love. But I promise thee, ye will be safe and our babe too!"

Robbie held her and led her inside the cave where a small fire burned in a little braiser. A pot of water was boiling on top and Robbie didn't say anything as he ladled tea measured with his hand into the little brown ceramic teapot that Lisbeth had brought him in order to have a proper cup of tea. She went to the makeshift shelf that held a couple of mugs and a simple pewter plate and returned to the table. It was cozy in the cave and Robbie was as comfortable as he could get under the circumstances. There was warm fur pelts laying across the large homemade, down mattress, stuffed by her own hand and brought to him in the dead of night when no prying eyes could see. They made love in the soft comfort of the downy bed and many a night she stayed snuggled and close to her Robbie, only to sneak out and back into her cold bed at dawn.

"Tis difficult I know, my dear but until I receive a pardon from King George I must live as a hunted man. Make no mistake about it, Lisbeth. The Captain who roams and raids the crofts means to round up all of us who were sympathetic to the cause. Your father's role in the uprising reflects badly on this Croft and capturing me would be a feather in the Captain's cap. Ah do. He'll no give up! I fear that daily I'll hear his step on the rocky path to this sanctuary." Robbie sat heavily on the small stool and frowning poured them builder's tea, strong and hot. Lisbeth joined him on the other stool and opened the small bundle which held a fresh wedge of goat's cheese and a large crust of warm bread. There was a hot pasties pie of meat and vegetables that Hallie Ross had prepared. Hallie had taken over the scullery and cooking duties when old Mother Ross had turned up her toes ten years before Lisbeth had come with her family to Brindle Hall as refugees after her Da had led the rebellion at Culloden and had suffered the ax at the tower of London a year ago. When she had commented that Lisbeth was eating for two she laughed. Lisbeth couldn't hide her condition from Hallie, but only William knew that Robbie was still close by. Lisbeth was three months gone with Rob's babe. This was the urgency that drove her. She wanted to be wed properly to her laird before her bairn came in December sometime before the winter solstice.

"With King Louie protecting you we could be married as well. I really think we need to get ye out of here until the King either pardons you or time allows an amnesty for the Highlanders. This can't go on forever, my love." She reached across the table and clutched his hand. "Please Robbie I talked to William. He is getting a shipment of whiskey ready to take to France. King Louie has ordered it. He leaves tonight. I fear so for you and our bairn. Will you go with William tonight?" Lisbeth looked up at Robbie and her gray-green eyes pleaded with him to relent and leave Brindle Hall to be safe. Robbie stared back at her his green eyes a match for hers. He ran his fingers through his curly raven black hair and his mighty chest heaved a sigh of resignation.

"We will take a wee peek at the tea leaves and see what they have to say." Robbie always knew he had a bit of his mother's gift of the sight. However, it only came to him when he needed to make a major decision in his life and the tool that seemed to work the most was reading the tea leaves as his Ma taught him.

Robbie drained his cup and then turned it upside down on the saucer and turned it three times. As he was about to turn it up he looked up and smiled at Lisbeth and she breathed deeply holding her breath as she awaited the revelation of the tea.

"Well, my dear, I see a sea voyage ahead and then it looks like I will see the King, see the crown there at the edge of the cup! But the question is, which King? Our friend King Louie of France, or our foe King George of England? Tis un-clear." Robbie frowned in concentration and turned the cup here and there to see if more was revealed.

"My love, as much as I want to stay here I will do as ye say and leave with Willie tonight. After all a good sea voyage will put me right. I've grown pale and thin living in this dark cave. The voyage will be a tonic."

Lisbeth embraced Robbie in Joy. Oh Robbie. I know it will be good for ye. I'll be grateful that ye be safe. King Louie will keep ye safe and I'll write ye of the doings at Brindle Hall. Ye will tell me exactly what ye wish us to do while ye are gone, I promise that we will do all that ye deem necessary to run the Hall." Lisbeth smiled broadly and couldn't contain the joy she felt. It was only then that she realized how worried she had been for her Robbie.

He reached for Lisbeth pressing his lips over her full sensual mouth and gripped her mass of auburn curls in his fist as he pulled her down to the pallet. The two stripped off their clothes frantic with want of each other and coupled together knowing that it would be their last until Robbie was free of the fear of capture. After a shuddering climax by both of them Robbie lay back on the pallet and held her close.

"Lisbeth, when I leave now who will see to Brindle Hall. We must stay in residence or the place will fall to wrack and ruin."? He looked down at his cup and stared at the murky depths. It was times like this he wished he had his mother's skill of prophecy to see the future. But Lady Eugenia had not used her skills for good. In her old age she became a jealous spiteful woman and used her black arts to try to destroy Lisbeth. In the end Eugenia died and Lisbeth had sent her to her death, challenging her in the small attic room and backing her against the balcony bannister, which she toppled over and fell to her death last spring. Robbie had mourned the mother of his boyhood, however, he didn't regret her death, and the old crone had become a threat to all that he loved.

"I will work with your Foreman Frank Gordon, with the help of William and my Ma. My Ma has taught me well. She taught me the healing arts of midwife and how to run a household and keep the accounts. I would be a good manager, in fact while you are in hiding that is how we are operating at Brindle Hall now. The tenants have planted the potatoes that you brought with Frank's supervision and we will have a full root cellar with the carrots, onions, and turnips as well. The goats have provided us with cheese and the chickens are laying abundantly. Tis true the strange color of their eggs puts off cook. But I've brooked no nonsense from her that the Black Copper Maran chickens were supernatural. Tis their eggs' rich chocolate brown shell that she objects too. Aye Robbie with ye in France ye would be a great help to your friend King Louie as you have been throughout this conflict. I will visit ye every forte night when William takes the whiskey and spirits to market." Lisbeth stopped talking out of breath from her long speech.

Robbie stood with his back to her and finally Lisbeth seeing his body sag she knew that she had won. He turned to her and held her close. " Lisbeth the child will show soon, what will you say when Lord Snowdon questions ye on how you became with child with me nowhere around?"

Lisbeth had thought this through and had hesitated to share her plan with Robbie for fear her would balk at it. "I'll tell him I was raped by a band of soldiers passing through after I gave them food. They crept up to the barn where I was milking and threw me into the hay! Robbie, the spoils of war, rape and plundering are common occurrences and women are not safe from it. It will work I say."

"I'll remind Hallie and William of the day the soldier's came and tell them the same story. By saying it happened in the barn and to spare them I didn't tell anyone until my belly grew . I've even told my Ma the same story and she believes me. She is a strong woman and after losing Da she's gotten stronger yet. She will vouch for me to Lord Snowdon."

Chapter 32

Robbie and Lisbeth spent the day together loving and making plans. Knowing that their lives were changing and Robbie's leaving was the only way to save his life. Lisbeth stayed with him until it was time to milk the goats then she went by way of the sea path down to the barns. She met William at the barn feeding the goats and starting to milk.

"There you be, Miss. I've started the milking and there tis only Josephine and Patsy left to milk. "William stopped talking as Lisbeth motioned him to silence and then whispered the plan Robbie had agreed to.

"So William, go to the schooner. Get the crew together. You leave at midnight. Robbie will be waiting. Go quickly. Tis much to do to be ready in time. Take the Polly Bee out beyond the breakers and wait until moon rise. I'll not want you here in case Lord Snowdon makes an appearance harassing and bullying everyone to tell him where Robbie be. I'll finish the milking, and set Hallie to cooking. I'll bring the food down at moon rise to the cave for Robbie to bring it with him."

Now that Lisbeth's plan was actually in progress she shuddered with fear that Lord Snowdon would come before Robbie could escape. The animal's warm presence eased her and she was grateful to be tending them. Finally she finished with Josephine and Patsy and patted their gray heads in thanks for not only giving her a full bucket of warm goat's milk but soothing her nerves as well. Lisbeth hurried out of the barn and just as she walked into the Hall she heard a clatter of horse stopping in front of her gate.

Quickly she took the milk to Hallie and called to her mother and Letitia to come join them in the kitchen.

"Ma Ma, Letitia, come quickly the soldiers are back!" The three hurried toward the kitchen.

Her sister Letitia, frowning and protesting the interruption to her reading pouted as Lisbeth, Clarise, Hallie and Letitia gathered around the scrubbed pine table. The women were busy and covered with flour by the time the English forced their way into the Hall. Old Moses, backed away from the front door as they shouldered their way into Brindle Hall.

"Where is your Mistress?" The tall Englishman barked at Moses who bowed deeply and motioned to the back of the house where the women were busy making biscuits and stirring the hearty Scotch broth that Hallie had made for dinner. Old Moses hands shook as he pointed toward the back of the house. His red whisker's and hair masked most of his expression, but his blue eyes were like flint. Standing only a little over five feet tall, bowlegged and beer-bellied, he knew he was no match for the King's men. He bowed deeply and backed away from them, cursing himself for his cowardice.

Lord Snowdon paused in the doorway. Flat bellied he cut a slim figure. His steel blue eyes and flop of brown hair gave him a boyish look until he pushed up his hair revealing a saber sword slash over his left eye. Addressing Lisbeth's mother as the eldest women present, he mistakenly took her for the Mistress of the manor. Lisbeth didn't correct him.

"Madame, I would be grateful to partake of that delicious broth. My men and I have been living on soldier's fare for far too long. The smells from this kitchen have clenched my stomach and reminded me that I've not had such fare in a forte night." Lord Snowdon bowed low to her and Clarise bowed in return, her back stiff, knowing that this was an order not to be refused.

"I bid ye welcome sir. If you will go to the dining room I will see to your meal. Hallie and Lisbeth go set the table while I finish the biscuits." The women bustled out to the dining room tense and mute. They went about setting the table as quickly as possible. Lisbeth spread a white linen cloth fresh from the laundry and ironed crisp over the large dining room table, while Hallie quickly put pewter plates and bowls, silverware and mugs for ale. There were five soldiers in all and all Lisbeth wanted was for them to leave as soon as they had their biscuits with fresh butter and Scotch broth. Clarise came behind them with a pitcher of cold Ale from the creamery. "Will ye have ale, my Lord?" Lord Snowdon nodded.

The women scurried back into the kitchen and not daring to close the door, busied themselves darting worried glances at each other. How were they going to get them to go? The tension in the kitchen made their back rigid with fear and Lisbeth motioned them to keep busy and stay silent. She pulled herself together and went back into the dining room just as Lord Snowdon pushed away from the table and wiped his mouth on the snowy white napkin.

"Now Miss. McIntosh, I ask you again where is your Laird Robert Alexander Fraser?" His fair skin reddened by the sun made his piercing blue eyes stand out in a no nonsense stare directly at Lisbeth.

Lisbeth curtsied to the soldier and met his gaze direct without flinching. "My Lord, I know not where Laird Fraser be. We've not had word of him since last Spring when he buried his ma, Lady Eugenia Fraser and left within the forte night. We've not had word of him since."

Lord Snowdon ordered his men to search the Hall. "Search every room, barn and stable!" The men scraped their chairs back and two headed toward the attic where Lady Eugenia had practiced her black arts. Thank heavens Lisbeth had emptied the attics of all her potions and buried them deep in the cemetery where Eugenia lay. Now the attic served as storage of her mother's remedies, dried herbs and ointments for healing only and Lisbeth faced Lord Snowdon with confidence that he would find nothing to betray Robbie. The men returned from their search and shook their head. Lord Snowdon fisted his hand and slammed it on the table causing the pewter dishes to crash to the floor. Lisbeth held her head high and didn't flinch as the man rose up in his chair, grabbed her by the arms, and shook her. "I'll make you watch as I strip him naked and whip him till his back runs blood. "Lisbeth stared up at the tall slender man in his Lobster back redcoat and white breech's and stood silent. With her silver- green eyes flashing defiantly. The Lord red-faced and stiff with anger yelled to his men to get going. "I'll be back, Miss McIntosh. You can't hold out forever and if I find that ye have aided him in any way, I'll thrash ye within an inch of your life, I will." With that he turned and stomped out of the Hall with his men trailing behind him. They mounted, lashed their horses and headed back out to the road.

Lisbeth and her mother breathed a sigh of relief. Clarise looked warily after them before she motioned her daughter into the small sitting room and closed the door.

"Lisbeth, you must leave with William tonight and take Letitia with you. Your babe will show soon and this man is crazed to find Robbie. I'll stay with Hugh. With the help of Hallie, Frank and Moses we can run the Hall. The tenants will help with the plowing and the crops. Now go hurry and pack what you both will need. I fear for your life. Take Letitia with ye. She is of an age to be used by such an angry man. I'll not see her raped. Go to our friend King Louie. He will find a place for you both in the palace."

"Oh Ma!" Lisbeth cried and went to her mother and Clarise opened her arms to her daughter and the two cried together. After wiping their eyes, Lisbeth left the little sitting room and called to Letitia. The two sisters went up to their room and hurriedly packed. Letitia, with eyes puffy and red, sniffed and began to pout.

"Lisbeth I'm so frightened. Why did Da have to go with Prince Charles? Why do men love war so much? What's to happen to us?" Letitia sat hard on the bed and began to wail.

Lisbeth gathered her into her arms. "There, there, we're going to be fine. We're going with William tonight to France. Ye like France and King Louie's court! We'll be safe there. King George will soon give up punishing the Highlanders and let them go back to their crofts. I promise ye it will be all right." Lisbeth stood up and briskly resumed packing.

Chapter 33

The moon shone bright as Lisbeth and Letitia walked quickly down the path to the lagoon where the Polly Bee was anchored. The sisters had said their good byes to their Ma, Hugh and Hallie. Hallie and Moses had bundled up enough food for the trip across the channel to France and safety for Robbie. It was a somber group that met on the deck of the schooner. William looked up with surprise to see Letitia and smiled. She blushed and was thankful that it was moonlight, hoping the shadows covered her redness. Lisbeth wasted no time in words and the schooner cast off and headed out to the breakers.

William's first mate launched a small rowboat and rowed to the tiny dot of light that Rob had lit to guide them in. It was quickly done. Rob was boarding the schooner in mere minutes.

Lisbeth rushed to his side and flung her arms around him.

"Lisbeth, what are you doing here?" Robbie sputtered in surprise.

Lisbeth put her fingers over his lips and hushed him. "I'll tell you all about it. Let's go below to our cabin so we can talk privately." She turned and led the way down the ladder to the staterooms and the large, comfortable cabin at the back of the ship.

The cabin door was no sooner closed when Robbie grabbed her and bid her explain.

Lisbeth turned away and looked out the porthole. The moonshine on the sea was beautiful. Finally she began.

" Lord Snowdon and his band of marauders rode into the courtyard, forced their way into Brindle Hall and demanded to know where you were. Oh Robbie, he threatened me with a thrashing. Ma is terrified that he will rape Letitia and use her in revenge for not telling him where you are. We talked about it. Ma urged me to go and take Letitia with me. She has a good plan on how to manage the Hall. Ma ran our estate in England so well that Da could be gone for months for the Cause. Da and Prince Charles often rode together gathering McIntosh's and clansmen to his cause.

Robbie considered this latest crisis and quickly made a decision. "Fay tis a mighty problem we have my dear. I'll take you to Mother Superior Agnes Scarholt to care for you and Letitia until William and I deliver the whiskey to King Louie. "

Lisbeth started to protest and Robbie lifted his hand to stop her." Nay, my Leamenn, I'll not chance the wagon trip to Versailles and you far gone with my babe. Nay my Leamenn, you'll wait for me with the good Sisters of Charity. I'll have peace knowing you and your sister are safe and our babe too."

Lisbeth knew that he wouldn't budge and finally she sighed and nodded.

Far into the night the schooner rode the sea through the deep swells and inside the Captain's cabin Lisbeth and Robbie slept through the night. They were unaware that in a small cabin at the far end of the ship where Williams cabin was, William and Letitia explored each other's bodies, thrilled to couple at last. It was dawn before the two slept. As the sun crept over the horizon Letitia tiptoed out of William's cabin down the corridor to her tiny cabin and went to her bed with a smile on her face.

The schooner reached the harbor town of Calais, a short trip of three days from Brindle Hall in the Highlands of Scotland. Captain Rob stood on the deck and guided his vessel into the port while the sailors scrambled to haul in the sails just in time for the ship to come to a slow halt at the dock. Sailors scrambled off the deck to tie the schooner to the dock while Rob surveyed the port from the deck. It was in deep shadow. Only the fishing skiffs had lights showing. He could smell fresh coffee brewing. After the ship was tied securely he left the deck to go into the galley where the cook, a mere lad, straight from his bunk, yawning mightily, was busy serving warmed - over stew and biscuits. Robbie tucked into his dinner and enjoyed the rich strong coffee laced with cream and honey.

Lisbeth and Letitia joined him for dinner. Lisbeth couldn't help seeing how Letitia and William were giving each other cow eyes. She stirred her coffee and looked worried.

Chapter 34

The schooner had docked at Calais shortly before evening tide. The runabout carriage that was kept on the ship for travel when on land was moved to the road by the dock, two matching roan horses that were stabled on the top deck under the bridge of the ship, were gently guided down the plank and hooked up to the lightweight carriage.

Lisbeth, Letitia, Will and Rob climbed into the carriage. In mere minutes the carriage was careening down the road toward the Sisters of Charity mother house, deep in the countryside outside Calais.

It was pitch black when the carriage pulled into the courtyard of the Abbey. Rob went to the door of the mother house. The door was massive with huge iron hinges on a thick plank door. He knocked briskly. Mother Superior, Agnes Scarholt opened the door herself.

"Bonjour Milord Rob. To what do we owe the pleasure of your visit to our humble home?" Sister Agnes smiled warmly. She looked past Rob to see two ravishing redheads being handed down by Willie from the carriage.

"Oui! You brought Lady Fraser with you but who is that lovely young lady with her?" She beckoned to the trio to join them inside. Lisbeth curtsied and kissed the Mother Superior's ring Letitia stood wide- eyed in the entrance and looked over at the gothic hall of arches that led into the depths of the foyer.

"Mother Agnes, this is my sister, Letitia McIntosh. We are in need of Sanctuary from the British." Lisbeth Looked straight into Mother Agnes eyes and held her breath, not letting it out until she saw the faint nod. Mother Agnes grinned and became her brisk self again. "Come, come, it is supper time. Sister Bernadette will bring you and your menfolk your dinner."

The Sisters who numbered twenty sat quietly at the long trestle table were forbidden to speak during their meal.

Mother Agnes led the group into a private dining room and bid them sit down. She clapped her hands and roly-poly Sister Bernadette entered with an urn of soup. She set the urn down on the table and passed the bread. Rob led Mother Agnes aside and whispered in her ear.

"Mother Agnes, I have need of your priest tonight. Lady Fraser and I are hand-fast and I wish to have our union blessed by a priest. We can't wait for the priest to come to

Brindle Hall. Lady Fraser is with child and I don't wish to leave her without the protection of my name as I will be away for a long time.

Mother Agnes nodded and turned to Sister Bernie and whispered in her ear. She glanced shyly over at Lisbeth . Mother Agnes turned back to Robbie and Lisbeth and grasped their hands in joy. "Oh children we all will keep you in our prayers." She had a big smile on her face as she made haste to prepare for the impromptu wedding.

Robbie and Lisbeth went back to the cottage to prepare for their nuptials. Letitia would serve as her attendant. William would be best man. Lisbeth scurried around the room unpacking her large trunk.

Lying across the top of the more serviceable clothing was a vision of a dress of shimmering ice blue satin and lace. It had long sleeves with lace trailing from the cuffs and a deep cut bodice that showed her full and lush bosom. The dress was meant to wear at court but it would make a wonderful wedding dress. Letitia had a soft rose colored dress of a simpler design that looked charming on her. Letitia helped Lisbeth with her toilet and her hair, arranging a white lace kerchief over her head. She had brushed it till it shown burnished copper in the lamp lite.

Rob had a silver satin waistcoat and black breeks that stopped at his knees. He wore fine white hose with black shoes decorated with silver buckles. William was dressed with a brown waistcoat and breeks and white hose with brown shoes. When Sister Bernie came for them and knocked quickly on the door, Lisbeth turned to Robbie and reached for his arm. They walked arm in arm through the garden and into the small chapel lite with creamy beeswax candles. The nuns were humming quietly as Robbie and Lisbeth walked to the altar where a chubby priest stood waiting in his simple brown robe and rope sash. Mother Agnes stood to one side and William and Letitia stood on the other side of the joyful pair.

The priest, Father Benedict, launched right into the simple marriage vows, "Dearly beloved, we are gathered here tonight to join Lisbeth McIntosh and Laird Robert Fraser in marriage....." In seconds the ceremony was over and Robbie was kissing his bride.

Mother Agnes poured a cup of claret for the priest and the wedding party. It was done.

Lisbeth and Robbie didn't get much sleep that night. They whispered their joy and happiness. When they heard William start to snore and the little snorts that

Letitia made, they made quiet sweet love on their side of the curtain. It seemed just minutes before there was a knock on the door and Sister Bernie came bustling in with hot tea and bread and cheese for their breakfast. After breakfast they stood by the carriage saying their last good byes. Mother Superior Agnes, hastened out of the Abbey in time to say goodbye to her friend Rob. Rob, kissed her ring and briskly kissed Letitia and gave Lisbeth a long sweet kiss lingering with regret at having to leave his new bride so soon after their wedding. She hugged him tight while he whispered in her ear, "I'll be coming to get you soon my dear wife. This is just a short separation." He turned back to the Sister and said,

"I am thankful that ye have room enough for both of these ladies until I can return for them". He paused an stuttered over "My wife and I" but plowed on to express their gratitude for the Mother's Superior's help to see them married.

Mother Superior smiled brightly and quickly nodded her head. "Of course we do, Rob. I look forward to the pleasure having Lady Fraser and Mademoiselle McIntosh with us for as long as is needed. Lady Frazer's gift with healing and herbs will be a great help to us." Rob jumped into the carriage and William gave the horse's free rein as they cavorted down the lane and headed back to Calais where they would switch the carriage for the now fully loaded wagon for the trip to the castle.

Sister Bernadette appeared and led the sisters back at the bottom of the garden where their safe snug cottage waited. The air was filled with the freshly turned earth, a pungent smell of soil and earth worms. Lisbeth looking after her husband's dust as it disappeared around the bend suddenly feared for him. She clung to Letitia and together gently moved toward the cottage. Mother Agnes followed the women in and Lisbeth turned to sob in the Mother Superior's arms.

Lisbeth and Letitia were distraught and Mother with the help of Sister Bernie coaxed them back to bed, tucking them gently under the soft down filled comforter . It was past noon when the two emerged from their beds and though pale and sad, walked through the garden and over to the tea table that Sister Bernie had prepared for them. As they drank their tea and ate the croissants with honey and butter, they looked around at the lovely garden. They looked forward to helping in the garden and inspecting the newest herbs that Sister Bernie cultivated.

The rest of the day was spent unpacking their trunks and tiding up the cottage. Lisbeth made the double bed behind the curtain and Letitia made up the small single bed in the alcove. The trip had tired them out. After a luncheon of cold meats and warm fresh bread and hot tea the two retired to their beds and slept till just after evening tide when the bell rang for evening chapel. Lisbeth and Letitia left the cottage to pray for their men surrounded by the comforting presence of the nuns and the soft light of the beeswax candles. They left the chapel as silently as the nuns and when they returned to their cottage the found a pot of tea and a sandwich made of rough ground wheat with sweet butter and creamy goat cheese. Exhausted from her emotional parting from Rob, Lisbeth crept back into bed and Letitia blew out the candle by her bed side. In moments they were fast asleep.

Chapter 35

The clanging of the bells again at dawn startled Lisbeth awake and for a moment she didn't know where she was. Then as she lit her candle and looked around the tiny cottage a rush of memory hit her. To keep from crying out, she stuffed her hand in her mouth and composed herself. When she felt like she could speak without sobbing she briskly called to her sister.

"Get up, Letitia. It's time for morning prayers. Let us join the nuns and pray for the safety of our men, it'll be daylight soon." Letita snorted and sat up looking dazed as she adjusted from sleep to wakefulness. It was only when Lisbeth saw Letitia stir toward her clothes that she turned back to the curtained partition and found her gold cross, Robbie's wedding gift to her, and slipped it around her neck. Lisbeth held the little cross and remembered Robbie's quiet words to her while they still lay snug in their bed yesterday morn. "I'll be back." She relived their wedding and then felt the shock wrench her as she remembered their abrupt departure at dawn. After dressing the two sisters hurried to the chapel for morning prayers.

It was full light in the chapel when Lisbeth opened her eyes again with a sunbeam beaming through the small windows and straight into her eye. She had prayed earnestly for her Rob's safety and the murmuring of the nuns saying the Rosary jerked her awake. She must have dozed. The nuns were leaving the chapel and Letitia squeezed her hand and looked worriedly at her. "You fell against me and I held you up, but I could see that you were asleep. Come Sister, let's go back to the cottage." The two walked quietly back through the garden and to their little temporary home. Lisbeth sighed and looked around the room. It was much nicer than it revealed last night with only one lantern to see by. There was a small writing table and lamp as well as a small stove with fresh wood and kindling next to it. She was thankful to see a small tea kettle and a pitcher of water. Lisbeth knelt down by the stove and fed some kindling into the banked fire, blowing on it until it caught in a blaze. She fed the tiny fire with more kindling and then added thin sticks until she had a blaze big enough that a small log wouldn't quench the flames. It only took moments for the water to heat. Peeking into the small brown teapot she noted the fresh tea waiting in the bottom. The fragrance of the tea as she poured boiling water in was swirling up toward her nose. Lisbeth let it steep then poured herself a cup of the brew.

"Ah it's lovely. I thank ye sisters for your forethought." Lisbeth went to the window an peeked out at the garden. She opened the cottage door and leaned out for a better look. It was newly weeded with young green shoots springing up along the rows. Lisbeth saw comfrey for wound healing and in the Middle Ages was a famous remedy for broken bones.

Lisbeth was grateful to see Penny Royal, a member of the mint family. If Letitia and Will were up to what drove young people, an she missed her courses, Lisbeth could make a tea that would bring on her courses. Lisbeth could smell the mint like leaves and the lovely purple flower which would bloom in the last half summer. Lisbeth picked enough for a pot of tea and set it to dry on a stone in the garden. 'I won't wait till she misses her courses, Lisbeth thought she shall have the tea tonight'. Lisbeth would be sure to gather enough for not only feminine needs but the plant also serves as wound cleaner and applied to cuts, wounds and the like, to be used to cleanse them and promote healing. Peppermint also grew freely in the garden it would come in handy to quiet a nervous stomach. Lisbeth used peppermint to help with her morning sickness and absently as she walked among the garden she plucked a stem and stripped the leaves before putting them in her mouth. She still had a bit of queasiness when she first awoke in the morning. There were so many plants in the kitchen garden that Lisbeth found a treasure where ever she looked. It was especially helpful to see Shepherd's purse so named because of the small pouches used for the seed of the plant that resembled a small, flat, leather purse. It's one of the most effective herbs for the treatment of bleeding. Lisbeth's mother Clarise used it in her midwifery. It has come in handy often when a young mother was hemorrhaging. It was one of her mother's trusted herbs when anyone of them had diarrhea.

Lisbeth was returning from the garden when she saw Sister Bernie coming from the kitchen with a laden tray covered by a white, freshly- ironed linen towel. Lisbeth held the door open and out of breath the stout nun hurried inside and placed the tray on the small round table that would serve as their dining area.

"There ye be, Lady Fraser." Lisbeth startled at the use of the title and then smiled as she realized that now she truly was "Lady Fraser".

"Thank ye sister. It smells delicious. Would ye be working in the garden today?" Sister Bernie busily set the table and spooned out the hot beef broth and poured the tea before looking at Lisbeth and nodding shyly. "I've a mind to get my hands in your wonderful French soil." Lisbeth said and smiled as Sister Bernie bowed her way out of the tiny cottage. When the good sister had left Lisbeth quickly drank her cup of tea and then sprinkled the half dried Penny Royal into the little teapot, pouring fresh hot water from the kettle on the braiser which kept the kettle hot all afternoon. The Penny Royal steeped and Lisbeth was careful to sip her tea as Letitia came to join her for dinner. Lisbeth watched her little sister in satisfaction when she had a second cup.

"Lisbeth, this tea is very good. I'd like some more for breakfast." Lisbeth smiled and nodded "of course Letitia you can have as much as you want. I myself prefer simpler fare, but I'll brew it for ye myself."

It was only a short week later that Letitia was looking around for some cloth to make a rag to catch her flow. Lisbeth sighed in relief and while she had the opportunity she picked as much as she could, without calling undo attention to her squirreling the precious tea away for future need. Lisbeth sighed she knew she couldn't keep Letitia and William apart now that they had begun to know each other so intimately. But she, by God, could keep the results of a babe from impacting Letitia's life at least until she reached her fifteenth year at the end of the year and they could be wed. Letitia was so young and such a child. Lisbeth would do everything she could to prolong her childhood.

Chapter 36

September

The days flowed into themselves the garden was beginning to produce. Lisbeth and Letitia busied themselves helping Sister Bernie weed the garden, a job which left them with sore backs, but helped to pass the long tedious waiting for Robbie. Lisbeth was beginning to show she was going into her fifth month and her morning sickness was now gone. Every day Lisbeth wished Robbie would come to fetch them. As Lisbeth finished her weeding, she looked up to see their carriage careening into the courtyard with only William aboard. Lisbeth knew immediately that something had happened and threw down her shovel, while racing to the gate. She called to Letitia to come but didn't wait for Letitia who didn't rush for anyone. It only took her a moment to reach the gate. Hurriedly she unlatched it and stepped into the courtyard. The carriage had come to a stop and the lathered horses were breathing hard. Lisbeth frowned, it wasn't like William or Rob either to abuse the horses like this.

"William! Where is Laird Rob?" William, looked down at his feet and then sighing looked straight into her eyes.

"It was a long month of Rob's meetings with the King. I think he kept us there purposefully because he enjoyed Rob's company, but finally we were off. We were laid upon one day out from the palace. Four big burly men pounced upon us in the dark and knocked me out. When I came to myself again my Laird was gone and I was left with only one horse and the empty wagon. I went back to the palace and they tended my wounds and sent scouts out to hunt for Rob. They found out that the men that had ambushed us were King George's men and that they boarded a ship in Paris bound for England. I hurried to yea as fast as I could. He broke down and Lisbeth hurried to his side and the two cried together.

"William we must ride to the King and beg him to intercede for Rob." Lisbeth turned and ran toward the cottage. She began to throw her clothes into a satchel. William trailed behind her.

"Oh no, My lady, ye mustn't. Ye know the king will claim his right of ye if ye ask him for such a favor. "I'll go speak to the King in your stead." William kept pace with her as she flew around the room, packing. Just then Letitia came into the cottage. She had been helping Sister Bernie with the herb garden and her dress was streaked with dirt.

"William ye are back!" Letitia rushed to him and threw her arms around him. A look of pure joy swept over her. Lisbeth knew at once that her suspicions were correct and that the two were in love.

Letitia looked past William and looked puzzled. "Where is Robbie?"

Before William could answer her Lisbeth blurted out. "The English have captured him. I'm off to plead with King Louie to intervene in his behalf. "Her determined look brooked no argument and Letitia shut her mouth and stared at her sister.

Lisbeth went to the Abbey to tell Mother Agnes what had happened.

Agnes sat at the tea table and listened quietly to Lisbeth who was pacing the room as she talked.

"So, Mother, we are leaving today to get the King's help." Lisbeth, agitated and worried, wrung her hands too distraught to stop moving. She finally ran out of words and the Mother Superior calmly stirred her tea and considered. "Ye know that the King will expect payment of ye?" Ye know what that payment will be." Her bright blue eyes pierced through all of Lisbeth's defenses and Lisbeth collapsed into the nearest chair.

"I'll think of something Mother. I'll tell him I am with child. I'll offer him a lifetime of free shipments of his precious brandy that ought to mean more to him than a poke at my body." As she voiced her thoughts she rose determinedly. "Yes that's what I'll do. I know it will work it must!"

After sipping the last of her cup of tea Mother Superior again looked straight into her eyes. "Ye must leave your sister with us. She is a sweet morsel and the king would take her in your place."

Lisbeth nodded and quickly went to the kindly old nun embracing her and letting her tears flow.

"Go now child. " The Mother Superior rose up to her full height and gently urged Lisbeth to hurry.

Lisbeth wiped her face with the tea napkin and quickly left the room. She sat Letitia down on the bed that had been Letitia's while she was at the Abbey and spoke quietly to her. When Letitia realized that she was to be left behind she jumped up an pleaded to go. Just then William came into the room and Letitia ran into his arms and poured out her frustration on him. Will pulled her away from him and lifted her face and softly said, "Your sister is right, ye would be in jeopardy if you went with us. I promise that as soon as we've spoken to the King, we'll come back and claim ye my little one."

Chapter 37

It was a tearful parting with Letitia begging to come. Both William and Lisbeth had to harden their hearts and left her crying at the gate with only the comfort of Sister Bernie to fold her into her arms and lead her back to the cottage.

Lisbeth watched the dusk turn to pitch black as the carriage flew toward the palace. No stops for comfort on this trip. Will lashed the horses and the carriage swayed dangerously as the horses galloped through the night. Lisbeth prayed that her babe would not be harmed by the trip, but it couldn't be helped. If they kept to this pace they would save a day's journey and arrive at nightfall tomorrow.

Chapter 38

Newgate Prison, England

It was dark in the dungeon and Rob didn't know where he was. He was shackled to the wall with only enough slack in the chain to reach his bed, the water bucket and the hole in the ground that stunk of shit and piss. Just above his bed there was a slit for a window. Rob carefully climbed up to see where he was, the chain bit into his wrists, but by craning his neck he could just see outside. The sight that greeted him made him break out in a cold sweat. A gallows stood right outside the window. Rob swallowed and looked around. He was in a prison that much was clear. Just then a gate below him opened to let in a wagon. Outside the gate Rob recognized the London Wall that surrounded the city of London. He was in England! Rob moved toward the water bucket and peered within. He wished he had his mother's powers. As he peered in he was surprised to see a mist forming in the water and coming up out of the bucket.

He stared in fright as the ghostly form hovered in front of him and became the shape and likeness of his mother, dead now over a year and buried at Brindle Hall. How could this be? I must be going crazy! Suddenly the apparition moved toward him and he felt her touch his hair and murmur to him as she had done when he was a wee boy.

"My boy, my boy. Do not fear me. Tis aye ye own mutter." Rob felt her grasp him to her and she felt whole and solid as she was before she died. Now he knew he was going crazy and he reeled away from her. "Ye are not real!" Just then in a split second his shackles were off his wrists and he was caught up in the mist. He looked hard at his mother as she calmly took his place, clamped the shackles around her wrists and to his horror turned into him. He/she smiled at him and with a sigh "died". Then he was whisked away in a swirl of cloud and deposited in a grove of gnarled trees away from the prison. He fell into a deep sleep. It was only when the morning dew fell over him waking him that he heard the drums beating. He looked over the crest of the small rise. He was well hidden in the scrub- like trees surrounding him and saw a plain wooden coffin being carried from what he now recognized as Newgate prison.

"My God tis not a dream!" Rob watched as the coffin was lowered into a hole and he heard his name spoken. Then wild with terror he looked around and saw the gnarled woods black with shadows and quickly half crawled away from the edge of the hill toward them. He struggled to get his bearings. He had passed Newgate Prison numerous times when he had gone to London on business with his father. It was a debtor's prison. But after the rising it was used for the war internment, as well some hardened criminals, felons, and filled with men, women and children who were housed there, innocent but too poor to pay their way out. It had a reputation for severe penalties and Robbie was astounded that with his ma's help he had escaped. He'd not think about what had happened. He'd just start running and get as far away from this awful place as he could get. Robbie took one last look at the scene of his burial and then crouched low and withdrew into the forest. There was a simple animal trail through the trees. His ma had made sure he was outside the London gate and Rob thanked her for it. The prison was one of the seven gates of the London Wall and Rob knew that a Roman road ran north past Christ Church.

Chapter 39

It was hard going through the dark woods full of brambles. Finally after three days and nights he came upon a small cottage. There was smoke coming out of the chimney. Rob watched and waited until he saw an old man with long white hair tied back in a low tail with a piece of rawhide, emerge and look right into the woods and beckoned him to come out. He smiled and opened his hands as if to assure him that he was not armed and it was alright to approach. Rob starving and cold walked slowly toward the old man and nodded toward him.

"I thank ye sir." He said as he moved toward the light of the cottage.

"Welcome traveler, I've a spare bed of straw if yea would like to come and rest a while. Ye look all tuckered, ye do." The old man held the door open and Rob grateful bowed deep to him, as he stumbled through into the warm, open one- room cottage. Rob looked around and saw the soup kettle on the hearth. It smelled wonderful and Rob's mouth began to water. Rob sat down where the old man indicated in front of the hearth, warm with hot embers radiating heat. He was able to nod again afraid of talking for fear he would give away his Scottish brogue. It's best if I pretend to be mute he decided.

"Come and sit here. I've pea soup, fresh bread and cheese. I don't get much company way out here and look forward to hearing the news." The old man bustled around . He didn't seem to mind that Rob hadn't said more than a grunt or two. Rob realized the old man might be deaf. He seemed to be happy to just gab away and didn't seem to require Rob to participate. Rob smiled at him as he set a bowl of steaming soup in front of him. The old man cut the bread, sliced the cheese and Rob ate his full.

After filling his belly and watching as the old man smoked his pipe, Rob yawned and stretched indicating he was ready for bed. The old man nodded and pointed to the loft above where a ladder led to a straw- filled space that served as insulation and helped keep the cottage warm. Rob again nodded and climbed the ladder. He was asleep almost as soon as his head hit the straw. The fact was he was almost mute with the shock of what had happened to him and he was thankful that he hadn't had to explain himself to the old man.

Chapter 40

Palace of Versailles

It took two nights for Lisbeth and William to reach the palace and another day before the King was free to see them. Lisbeth and William stayed in her father's old apartment, the one that he had used when visiting King Louie.

Lisbeth curtsied low to the King and Willie stood behind her and bent his knee showing his leg. King Louie nodded to them and bid them to come closer. Lisbeth was led to the small breakfast table where King Louie was finishing his own croissants. Finally he wiped his mouth and threw down his napkin.

"Lady Fraser, I'm afraid that I have received bad news. Please sit down." The king indicated a chair across the small table and looked sadly at Lisbeth." I received a letter from King George that your Laird Robert Fraser was found dead in his cell at Newgate prison two days ago." King Louie looked directly into her eyes and continued, "I'm sorry, my dear, but I have proof ." He drew out Rob's signet ring and handed it to her. "I gave it to him when he and young William were here a forte night ago. King George did not say how he was captured or how he came to be in that cell, but I believe him. I give you the ring now and hope it will serve you and take you to safety." He handed the ring to Lisbeth. As she held it in her hand her grief overwhelmed her.

Lisbeth swooned and if William hadn't been directly behind her would have crumbled to the floor. William caught her and lifted her easily. He bowed to the King and walked backward with Lisbeth in a deep faint in his arms.

He didn't turn until he was out of the king's presence. He saw the footman and hailed him. "You there, have our carriage and horses brought to the carriage door," he barked. Then he hurried back to the apartment where he deposited her on her bed. As she struggled to waken he rubbed her wrists and spoke urgently.

"My Lady, we must leave at once. We must go back to Brindle Hall as soon as we can. We'll pick up Letitia from the good Sisters and get back to the ship." He was packing her satchel as he spoke.

As Lisbeth carefully sat up on the bed, William handed her cloak to her. Lisbeth said nothing only stared at the ring so big that she had put it on her thumb. Her Robbie had worn this and now she would keep it as a talisman for safety for her and her babe as Robbie would want her too. Maybe it would someday help her child. She was in such deep shock that she couldn't think. William bustled around packing her satchel, then hauled her down the stairs to the carriage entrance.

"Come now, My lady." William half carrying Lisbeth down to the carriage and quickly deposited her inside, he nodded to the footman with his white wig and swung up to take the rains and they were off.

They, kept a steady pace only stopping to refresh themselves at taverns along the way. By night fall the second day they drew up into the courtyard of the Abbey. The door swung open and Mother Agnes stood peering out into the darkness holding an old lamp with a lit candle lighting the dark, as William climbed into the carriage and backed out carrying Lisbeth in his arms, as she had fallen into a swoon . Will carried her through the garden gate with Mother Agnes running to keep up.

Mother Agnes frowned at William and scolded him. "Ye stupid man. My lady is with child. Ye must allow her to rest before you continue your journey or ye will lose both of them." Agnes huffed as she swept out of the cottage. Letitia hurried to Lisbeth's side. Will gently put Lisbeth on the big bed she had shared with Rob on their wedding night and covered her with a blanket.

"Oh William, what's happened?" Letitia grabbed Lisbeth's hand and started to rub her wrist. William pulled her away and out to the garden and softly told her what had happened.

"Dead! How? When?" Letitia clung to William and began to wail. Will led her over to a stone bench in the garden and quietly told her .

"King Louie had his ring. Tis true, I'm sorry, but the laird is dead and now what is going to become of us all?"

"Letitia, with Rob dead, there is no one to protect ye and your family. I love ye so much and I can protect ye if yea will consent to marry me while we are here with the nuns"

William looked hopefully at her. Letitia looked up into his eyes trustingly and said "I love ye my William. Ye know that. I would be honored to be your wife."

Lisbeth slept through the night and all the while Letitia and Will were planning their future together. William had gone to the Mother Superior and requested a priest.

Letitia and Will stood before him with only the Mother Superior as witness. Letitia regretted that Lisbeth wasn't able to be there, but it couldn't be helped.

Chapter 41

Lisbeth opened her eyes when the sun streamed through the window and awakened her. Mother Superior was sitting next to her bed.

"Ye and your babe are well Lisbeth I'm glad to see ye awake. I've examined ye. Ye are doing well. I've news for ye. I do not wish to upset ye, but it must be told. While ye were recovering your man William and Miss McIntosh were married by the priest with myself as witness. No! Hold up now. William is right. Ye and your sister, and family are unprotected now that Laird Rob is dead. From all they told me this makes perfect sense. William can protect ye from that Lord Snowdon. I know when ye've time to think things through ye will be grateful for his help." She stopped talking and poured a cup of tea and handed it to Lisbeth who had managed to sit up against the pillows, her face as white as the cotton pillow cases.

Finally Lisbeth sighed "Mother Agnes, I've known that William and Letitia loved each other. I was hoping they would wait until the new year when she would be ten and five. She is so young." Lisbeth sipped her tea and then resigned to the fate accompli, put her tea cup on the table and pushed herself out of bed. She was a little wobbly and the good Mother Superior helped her to a chair.

After she was dressed she with the help of Mother Agnes walked into the garden where William and Letitia were waiting. They stood up when they saw her approaching. She motioned them back to their seats and took a small wooden stool next to them.

"Well, I hear congratulations are in order. I give ye both my best wishes, dear ones". She smiled and the tension between them was broken. Letitia stood and embraced her sister. William came over and the three hugged with tears all around. Will stood back and hugging Letitia looked square in Lisbeth's eye, "I promise ye, my dear sister that I will love and protect Letitia with my life, and yours, your Ma's, and little Hugh's as well. Think of me as your brother as Rob and I were brothers at heart. He'd want me to care for ye all."

Chapter 42

It was October before Lisbeth felt strong enough to go back to Brindle Hall.

The leaves turned yellow and some a deep red and the winds started blowing, setting their candle to waver while sending moving shadows on the walls of their snug cottage. William kept watch over the weather and finally came to speak to Lisbeth.

"The winds are here and if we want to get back to Brindle Hall before the gales start and churn the seas we best be going , My Lady." He looked hopefully at Lisbeth and she nodded.

"I agree William. Letitia and I will pack today and be ready at first light to go to the ship." William nodded and rushed out to tell Letitia. Letitia was in the garden pulling carrots for their stew with Sister Bernie. She looked happy and serene when William walked up to her.

"My love, we leave at dawn for the ship and the voyage to Brindle Hall. I've come to fetch you to help Lisbeth with the packing." Letitia rose, handed the carrots to Sister Bernie, and stepped into her husband's arms.

"Won't Ma and Hugh be surprised both her daughters being brides and she not part of it. We will have to break the news to her over those wonderful chocolates we got when we went to Paris last week."

Letitia sighed as she remembered their two day honeymoon while Lisbeth was convalescing. They stayed in the French quartier in an old hotel's particulars amid exclusive countryside-like hamlets. They dined on caviar and snails that Letitia wrinkled her nose at. But she loved the champagne! She was happy with good bread and cheese and all the champagne she could drink!

"Oh William, if only Rob was here I could celebrate as I want to. My poor sis, a widow before she was hardly a wife! And her with a wee babe coming. I just can't believe this has happened to her. She has worked so hard to take care of everyone and now she has no one to love." Letitia began to sob in William's arms.

" She has ye, your Ma, Hugh and me. Brindle Hall will be a haven for us all, I promise ye!"

Lisbeth finished her packing and left Letitia's for her. She was anxious to gather as many herbs as she could. Going out to the garden, she picked and sorted them until it was time for supper. Lisbeth was suddenly anxious to return to Brindle Hall. She busied herself packing the herbs she had carefully wrapped in paper and tucked them into her satchel. When she was ready she left the cottage and went to Mother Superior Agnes and the two closed the door to her study.

"Mother, here is some money for our care. I can't begin to thank you and your Sisters for ye love and care. Ye have saved me and my babe. I will be forever grateful . I ask that ye keep my babe in ye prayers that we have safe passage and that the babe is born healthy. I wish for a son for Rob's first and only child, but God will decree what emerges. Please pray for us that my labor will be short and the babe will live."

Mother Agnes nodded, accepted the money as the two knelt together in front of the personal altar and prayed together. Agnes gave her a tiny piece of bread and a small thimble of wine and they celebrated the Eucharist together.

After a last supper in the Abbey of a hearty stew and warm bread and cheese, the trio bid the sisters goodnight and retired to their small cottage. They were packed and their bags except for a small duffle of their night clothes were already stowed in the boot of the carriage. They would leave early in the morning.

There was a light tap on the door just before dawn. Sister Bernie had a tray with a pot of hot strong builder's tea and fresh bread and cheese. She also had a cloth bag filled with apples, cheese and bread and a flask of wine for their journey.

"Safe journey, Lady Fraser. I will pray for you every day of my life." Sister Bernie curtsied and bowed as she carried the empty tray back to the kitchen. Lisbeth, William and Letitia looked around the cottage and when they were satisfied that they had left nothing behind, hurried to the carriage and with a lash of the whip they were off. The horses, two brown mares, were fresh and eager to stretch their legs. It was all William could do to keep them to a trot as they wound around the narrow country lanes. It was difficult to see around the sharp curves and William reined the horses in whenever they came to one, to make sure they didn't run head on into another carriage or wagon.

Chapter 43

It was past noontime when they finally reached Calais after one night in the small but comfortable Inn on the road and boarded the Polly Bee. Lisbeth and Letitia went straight to their cabin, leaving William and a couple of the mates to load the horses and carriage and see to their luggage. All William had to do was pay the dock-keeper the docking fee. The crew had done quite well with young Ian Ross the acting first mate while William was gone. Fresh food of fruit and what vegetables that could be had such as onions, carrots and turnips had been purchased for the crews meals and with the salt pork stowed in plenty below they had enough to eat while waiting for William to return. Young Ian had them mending ropes and cleaning the ship from top to bottom. They were ready to sail immediately. Within the hour the schooner slipped out of its berth and headed north toward Scotland. The crossing and up the coast was unusually rough and the little ship battled the waves in full sail. Lisbeth stayed in her cabin until late that night and then she walked the deck finally standing at the bow of the ship facing the foaming waves as the ship dipped and rose its way up north toward Dornoth and the sanctuary of

Brindle Hall. She hugged her stomach as her babe pitched and rolled fluttering and kicking inside her while the seas outside steadily rolled in tandem with the babe in her womb. Lisbeth sighed, returned to her cabin and in minutes was sound asleep.

When Lisbeth awakened, she hurriedly dressed and went up on the deck. She saw the man at the wheel and for a moment caught her breath. "Rob! She whispered." But when she hurried toward the man he turned and it wasn't her beloved at all. It was William. He smiled at her and wished her "good morn."

Lisbeth nodded to William and went to the rail to watch the boat cut through the water heading toward Scotland. They were just out of sight of land but the clouds hovered over the land and Lisbeth could see the faint outline of the land as they sailed past. It was a relief that it was cloudy they wouldn't be so easy a target for the man of wars that the English patrolled the coast of England with. Only the cover of darkness or clouds could protect them.

Lisbeth sighed and walked to the galley where the young mate greeted her and beckoned her to sit down. He would bring her some tea. The kettle was kept full on the back of the stove and in just seconds he put a small brown teapot made of pottery in front of her with the tea steeping inside.

Breakfast was porridge and biscuits and butter with honey. It was simple fare but the heavy food helped her queasy stomach from rolling. The babe did enough of that without being seasick. Lisbeth was thankful that she had proved she was a good sailor when Rob and her Da took her with them to Culloden last year. Suddenly the memory of her father's beheading leaped into her mind and with Rob's death too, she collapsed in tears and shoved the food away from her. She lay her head on the table and sobbed. The little boy ran for William.

Chapter 44

Edinburgh Scotland

The old man told Rob that his croft was just outside the city of Edinburgh and Rob after days of helping him tend his animals, churn butter and make cheese felt that he could trust him. Rob told him that he was heading for his home near Dornoth, Scotland and he was escaped from Newgate Prison and certain death. Rob gave him a false name of Rob McIntosh and he didn't tell him any of the details of how he had escaped the English. The old man just nodded his head and with his easy manner conveyed that Rob was safe with him. No one came up his way, he said but if they did he'd tell them "That ye are my nephew." Jacob Duncan had fought in the rising, he had survived and hidden himself in this croft growing his hair long and pretending to be deaf. He tended to his own business and the hill folk accepted him and left him small gifts, but otherwise left him in peace. Jacob told Rob, he smiled broadly like it was a bit of a joke and his blue eyes twinkled as he chuckled to himself.

It was finally the winter solstice, in late December and Rob yearned to be home with Lisbeth. Rob had told Jacob that his wife was with child and Jacob watched Rob carefully as he went about his chores. He kept him busy and the chopping of firewood for the winter helped him work off his nerves.

The wind started blowing and the colors changed on the trees, deep gold and bronze leaves with streaks of red through them. The snow was falling steadily as Rob and Jacob hurried to feed the milk cow and sheep and a goat with her kid, trudging through the thick sloshy stuff, mixed with the colorful leaves. Jacob and Rob finished making butter and goat's cheese when a roar of wind with a heavy snow fall drove them into the cottage. They stoked the fire and Jacob put on pot of vegetables and salt pork. Soon the onions perfumed the air. Jacob tasted the soup and declared it ready. He ladled it into soup bowls and Rob cut chunks of homemade bread that Jacob baked every other day. To this they added fresh butter and the goat cheese and dinner was ready. The wind howled all night. It was a relief to go to bed and tuck in the straw with the sheep skin over him. Rob slept deeply.

In the morning it was still snowing. Jacob insisted on going out to feed the stock and Rob went with him into the heavy gray weather. They both were soaked through when they finally were able to go back inside and huddle in front of the fire till they were warm and dry. The rest of the day they busied themselves with making fresh bread.

Rob watched Jacob mix the flour and out of an old jug he put a cup of putrid smelling flour, yeast and water that he had let ferment. This he put in the bowl with the flour, lard and salt. He kneaded the dough and shaped it into round loafs that he let rise in a warm corner of the stove top. The resulting bread was delicious and now he had the secret to take home to Hallie. The days flowed together Rob and Jacob got along well and Rob began to relax. He had grown a bushy red beard and let his hair grow long till it too was long enough to be tied back with a piece of rawhide shoelace that Jacob gave him.

The cottage was the perfect place to disappear until he could resume his life at Brindle Hall. But Rob knew that it would be a long time. In the meantime winter was coming and Rob put out of his mind that the babe would be coming at Winter Solstice. Lisbeth was safer not knowing he was alive.

In the long late afternoons when they were finished with the chores, Jacob would tell Rob stories of the rising of

1715 when the Jacobite's were defeated by the English. Rob told him of the rising of 1745 when the Jacobite's were soundly defeated again and Scotland would never be the same. Jacob trusted Rob and he thought Rob would be a good shrine tender after his time. It seemed like the perfect solution. After thinking for several days how to approach Rob he finally just sat down and told him. Jacob knew that he was getting too old to take care of the shrine for the Old Ones much longer. He felt it in his bones that his time was coming.

It was at the end of the day that Jacob led him to the roadside shrine with the hollow bowl filled with dried fruits and a couple of copper coins.

"Rob, I tend the shrine of the Lady". Jake picked out the copper pennies and the dried fruit and put them into a satchel tied to his belt. "My father before me tended her and when he died I took over." Jacob looked up at Rob and smiled. The two turned back to the cottage and sat down in front of the small braiser as a chill wind had blown up while they were outside. Jake didn't say more . He put a pot of wild onion, carrots, turnips and other vegetables on top of the braiser and added the haunch of a rabbit. Rob put bowls on the table and a slab of fresh bread with sweet butter churned that morning .

The wind kept Rob awake with the shutters rattling and the chill in the air. Finally he got up and put fresh kindling into the braiser and a thick log when the fire had caught. Just then he heard a strangled grasp. Turning he peered over where the old man was sleeping. When Rob reached his bedside he saw the old man struggling to breathe. He raised him and added pillows to help him. Jacob took his hand and after a shuddering cough started to speak.

"Rob, will you tend the shrine for me? " He began to cough and Rob bent low to his ear.

"Old man, you'll be fine on the morrow. It's not your time yet . But if it will ease ye I promise ye I will tend the shrine until another keeper can be found. I thank ye for your help. Rob put the kettle on to steam and when it was hot made a pot of tea and fed it to him with a teaspoon. The tea seemed to comfort him and he breathed easier. Rob covered him and sat next to him holding his hand until he slept. When Rob saw that he was asleep he quietly moved away and put more logs on the fire before curling up in his straw bed and slept.

Chapter 45

It was morning and the first birds were stirring. Rob woke with a start. The cottage was very quiet. He came down the ladder and in the eerie stillness he knew the old man was dead, gone as lightly as a breeze, his bright blue eyes staring sightless. Rob closed his eyes and wrapped him in his Duncan plaid, a dark green with plaid of red, white and black that would be his shroud. Rob secured the plaid with Jacob's family Duncan crest badge of a ship under sail.

It took him most of the day to dig a grave behind the cottage croft and by early evening he had finished.

Throwing the last shovel of dirt over the simple grave, Rob lashed together a cross of tree branches and stuck it at the head of the grave. There was nothing left to do. A tiredness such as he hadn't felt before bore down on him and with a last look at the grave Rob went back to the cottage, stoked the fire and began to make tea. As he sipped his tea and ate his simple dinner of bread and cheese Rob brooded. Now that he was alone his rush of feelings for Lisbeth surfaced and he yearned for her with a desire that he had kept deep in his heart. A wild thought came to mind. Can I use the water to see her? If only I could see that she fared well, it would be enough. Rob rose and walked over to the water bucket. He peered down in to the bucket and at first nothing happened. He frowned and concentrated all of his love and yearning as he peered closer. Suddenly a misty cloud swirled in the bucket and as it quickly cleared to reveal Lisbeth bathing in their bedroom. She was naked with her copper hair brushed to glowing and trailing down her back and over her breasts her stomach huge with child. Rob realized that it would just be a few days until the babe came. He cried out her name and saw her start and look around the bedroom. 'My God, she can hear me!' He tried again. "Lisbeth, tis me, your Rob, come to your washstand and look in the basin my love". Lisbeth wrapped herself in a huge white towel and cautiously walked over to the water basin and peered down. Looking up at her was a black haired man with a great red beard. "Robbie? Ye have your mother's gift. Oh where are you, my love? I must be dreaming this, it can't be real, ye are dead! King Louie showed me your ring!" Lisbeth looked again and the image of her Rob was still there smiling a huge smile at her.

"Oh, my love, tis quite a story, but I can't tell ye now. I will tell ye where I am and all is well. "Rob told her about the shrine keeper's croft west of the Roman road from Edinburgh. As if in a dream Lisbeth wrote down his instructions and agreed to go to him. Before they parted, Rob told her he would visit her again in the basin every evening when she came to bed.

"Watch for me, my love, I'll never be far from you." Rob said as the basin water clouded up again and he was gone.

Lisbeth thought she might have been in a faint and dreamed the whole incident except that on the parchment was her careful notes of his location at the shrine.

That evening she felt her waters break . A gripping pain bent her over double and she didn't have breath to utter a sound. It was only when her mother came in to say good night that she was able with a quick glance at her daughter to see that she was in active labor.

Clarise examined her daughter probing her abdomen with a look of concern. "What is it, Ma?" Clarise looked hard at her daughter.

"The babe is breech. I must turn it." Clarise mixed a draft with a lacing of laudanum in it enough to dull what she was about to do but not harm the babe.

"Lisbeth, here drink this." She drank the tea with laudanum that made her drowsy and her mother bent over her daughter and with great skill turned the child to slip through the birth canal. Lisbeth's pains came stronger and before dawn her mother took from her body first a baby boy squalling, red-faced and fists waving and then a baby girl mewing like a kitten. All through the long night, Rob had been watching, listening, and praying for the safe delivery for his wife. He was overcome when he heard that twins had been born. The room was a bustle of activity with a lantern burning all night. With Hallie's help the babies were washed, dressed, and tucked into bed with Lisbeth. Rob turned away from the bucket and thanked God for their safe delivery.

Lisbeth was busy nursing and admiring her newborns. For the whole day she didn't think again of the strange message." No, Robbie was dead," she thought, "I've his children now to protect and raise." That night after the moon rose and crystals grew on her windowpanes, she was leaning over her basin when that strange murky cloud appeared again in the water and a smiling Rob appeared in the ripples.

"I was with you all night long, my love. Two healthy babes! No man could be richer! Lisbeth though startled to see and hear him speak, accepted that Rob had his mother's gift even stronger than his Ma's.

"I dinna think ye were real. Oh Robbie, tis true, ye are truly alive!" Lisbeth and Rob talked together making plans. When the candle started to gutter Lisbeth lit a fresh one and tiptoed to the babes' baskets and carefully brought first his son, quickly named " Robert Jerome", and then his daughter "Alice Elizabeth," over to the basin for their father to see them.

Chapter 46

Old Jacobs Croft

Robbie was finished with his milking and stall mucking. It was a clear cold January morning when he heard horses coming along the road leading to the croft. He glanced out to see his two roan horses and the wagon. Sitting atop the wagon was William. Robbie dropped his shovel and raced to open the gate. The wagon moved through the gate at a trot and William jumped down and embraced Rob. "William, tis good to see you man." Rob grinned at his best friend and then turned to the wagon reached up and took Lisbeth's arm and lifted her out of the wagon.

William had jumped back into the wagon and was gently leaning over a small open box with two small wee babes laying side by side snug in their warm nest. He carefully lifted out first the baby girl Alice Elizabeth, with her ruffled white cap and lay her in his father's arms and then quickly picked up the infant named after his father Robert Jerome called Robin by Lisbeth and their Grand mere Clarise. Gently Rob opened his other arm and held both of the babes, grinning with tears running down his face.

"Lisbeth, my dear, I dinna dare hope that we'd ever be together and now here yea are. Come inside it's cold out, the wee ones will be chilled. He ushered them into the warm cottage, then turned to William and his arms full with the twins he handed the babes to him and opened his arms to Lisbeth. Lisbeth felt his solid body and at last truly believed that it was her Rob.

The three spent the rest of the day talking. William was speechless and wistful as he watched Rob holding his son. William hoped that Letita would have a boy this first time, but it would be September before her time came. He sat and listened to Lisbeth and Rob. Lisbeth explained how they were able to leave Brindle Hall.

"Moses and Ma had us up and fed before dawn while the tenants were still abed. We had hidden the wagon in the barn. It was after I nursed the babes that we tucked them into the wagon and we were off with not a light showing in the croft. The babes slept until their next feeding and by then we were well on the road. I kept to the wagon with the sides down and closed. William wore an old hat like an old farmer going to Market day. We joined the other wagons making their way to market and then kept going taking back roads through Dornoth until we" Lisbeth stopped as Rob grabbed her and held her close. "Thank God ye are safe. William, I'm beholding to you, my friend." It was easier seeing Rob and William relaxed and Lisbeth sighed heavily.

"It was a rough week on the road pretending to be like gypsies but we dinna have any trouble from the English. They hardly gave us a look. Going through Edinburgh was the most nerve wracking, of course, with the troops stationed there because King George was in Holyrood castle. We kept our heads down and kept moving." William stopped in wonder that it was all true just as Lisbeth had told him that his Rob was alive and living as a hermit shrine keeper.

William's eyes filled with tears as Rob reached out and embraced him.

"Tis true, my friend. I owe ye for bringing me wife and babes to me, William. We are now true brothers, I congratulate ye and Letitia on your marriage and you're coming babe. Lisbeth told me how ye married while at Mother Agnes's to protect her and my family too. I can never repay your faithfulness." Rob smiled as William gasped when he realized that it was really true that Lisbeth and Rob had been communicating through the water in his bucket. It seemed incredible!

Lisbeth joined them in a group hug and then the three sat holding the babies while Rob cuddled first his son and then his daughter. They were miracles for sure. The three sat late by the fire making plans. William would act as Overseer of Brindle Hall and live there openly with Letitia, Clarise and Hugh. If Lord Snowdon asked where Lisbeth was he would tell him that she was with the Sisters of Mercy in the Mother house in France. Lisbeth and Rob would tend the shrine and stay hidden until the King saw fit to pardon the Highlanders, or Rob could take them all to King Louie in the Spring.

Later after the babies were tucked in their warm cradles, a present from their Da crafted carefully by the fire each night while he waited for Lisbeth to arrive.

The wind was up outside and with it a cold wet snow plopped softly against the shuttered cottage. Lisbeth and Rob were snug in their feather bed that Lisbeth had brought from Brindle Hall. William was up in the loft snoring loudly.

Lizbeth and Rob clung to each other and made slow sweet love, mindful of William's presence in the loft above them. Spent with emotion and ready to sleep the two

held tight to each other.

Lisbeth whispered to Rob, "Golden dreams, my love" and spooned against him. The magic of the night lulled them to sleep.

The End

A note from the author.

I hope that you have enjoyed my historical fiction of the beginnings of the Fraser family in eighteenth century Scotland. I began to think of Lisbeth's and Robbie's story after I wrote my contemporary novel Without Consent.

Without Consent is also about the Fraser family, however, it is set in the twenty first century, two hundred years removed from Lisbeth and Robbie's story. Now that I have written both of these novels I will be free to work on the rest of the series of the Fraser clan in my future contemporary novels. I will however visit Lisbeth and Robbie through their letters and journals that they left in Brindle Hall, the family home that still houses Fraser's to this day.

I love hearing from my reader's please e-mail me at vdiggy@att.net. In the subject line put the name of the book you would like to discuss either Fraser's Lady or Without Consent or my Haiku poetry books and I will open the e-mail and write back to you.

Virginia Degner

July 29, 2014 Castro Valley, California

About the author.

Virginia Degner was a reporter in the Bay Area writing feature stories for her local newspaper. Her love of writing evolved into writing a parenting web site for Parenting information after she retired from her work as a Social Worker specializing in foster care. Visit her website Theparentconnection.info .

Virginia has a master's degree in clinical psychology and has put her knowledge to work after retirement by developing her characters and themes using many of the resources therapist's use in their therapeutic environment.

Printed in Great Britain
by Amazon